I Have No Intention of Saying Good-bye

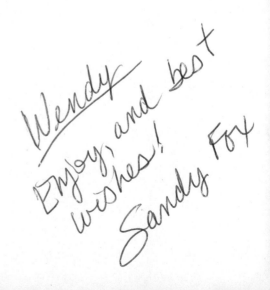

Wendy
Enjoy, and best wishes!
Sandy Fox

I Have No Intention of Saying Good-bye

Parents share their stories of hope and healing after a child's death

Sandy Fox

Writers Club Press
New York Lincoln Shanghai

I Have No Intention of Saying Good-bye
Parents share their stories of hope and healing after a child's death

Second edition 2005

Writers Club Press
an imprint of iUniverse, Inc.

iUniverse books may be ordered through booksellers or by contacting:

iUniverse
2021 Pine Lake Road, Suite 100
Lincoln, NE 68512
www.iuniverse.com
1-800-Authors (1-800-288-4677)

ISBN-13: 978-0-595-16118-8
ISBN-10: 0-595-16118-9

Printed in the United States of America

To Marcy, my precious daughter, and to all the mothers and fathers who have had to endure the death of a child.

We Remember Them

In the rising of the sun and in its going down,
We remember them;

In the blowing of the wind and in the chill of winter,
We remember them;

In the opening of buds and in the warmth of summer,
We remember them;

In the rustling of leaves and the beauty of autumn,
We remember them;

In the beginning of the year and when it ends,
We remember them;

When we are weary and in need of strength,
We remember them;

When we are lost and sick at heart,
We remember them;

When we have joys we yearn to share,
We remember them;

So long as we live, they too shall live,
for they are now a part of us as

We remember them.

from Gates of Prayer, Reform Judaism Prayerbook

About the Author

Sandy Fox

The publication of a poem by Sandy Fox at age five started her lifelong career in the writing field. While in high school and college she wrote articles for the school newspapers and yearbooks. She received both her B.A. and M.A. in Journalism. After college she worked for a daily newspaper as a news-feature writer.

A few years after daughter Marcy was born, Sandy decided to take what she knew how to do so well into the classroom. For 28 years she taught high school journalism and English and produced a state and national award-winning school newspaper. She spoke many times at national conferences and summer workshops for both teachers and students. Sandy also won many honors for her contributions to journalism and the teaching profession. She also found time to write one book and still freelances feature stories, travel book reviews and cruise reviews for travel magazines.

Four years after the death of her daughter, Sandy retired from teaching and began a two-year, non-fiction book project dedicated to Marcy, one that would tell the stories of grieving parents five years or longer after the death of their child and how these parents used a variety of techniques to move forward and enrich their lives while always remembering their child, as Sandy strives to do daily. She hopes these stories will honor those parents and be of help to those still having difficulty dealing with their loss.

Contents

4. Jennafer 86

A parent speaks to Victim Impact Groups about being responsible drivers. She believes it is only through education about the consequences that we can help these people.

5. Stephanie and Stephen 92

Parents speak of losing both children, decide they have enough love in them to parent two additional children and relate how this has affected their lives.

6. Sheryl 99

A daughter died at age 26 from the stomach flu. It turned out to be the first known recorded case of Salmonella poisoning. Through her death, her mother is comforted knowing many lives have been saved.

7. Craig 107

A mother unsuccessfully deals with her son's schizophrenia before his death from a self-inflicted gun shot. She now works for the Mental Health Association and tries to educate people so they won't feel the shame and stigma usually attached to mental illness.

8. Justin 115

Parents learn to accept their 16-year-old son's death by alcohol poisoning with the help of family members and by reliving only the good memories.

9. Jimmy 119

An accidental gunshot wound to the head shattered one family and the time that would have been spent with a son is devoted to helping others survive their grief through The Compassionate Friends.

10. Dusty and Afton 126

Parents must deal with the death of two children in one accident. Their faith, an organization for those who lose all their children, Alive Alone, and the adoption of a Korean child helps them.

19. Tommy and Paul Jr. 178

An airplane accident and a car accident end the lives of these parents' two sons. How they grieved differently, what it is like to have all your children taken from you and how they survive each day is what these parents talk about.

20. Aaron 186

A mother is torn apart by guilt when her son dies at a wilderness survival camp she forced him to go to because of his drug and related problems. She made a bad judgment, but at the time it was all she knew to do.

21. Peggy 194

A father attributes his clairvoyance to the fact that he knew his daughter would not survive her injuries. Through a self-realization group he and his wife learned to understand themselves and realized the power of the subconscious mind.

22. Jennifer 200

Parents lose their daughter from an illness but believe God has taught them tremendous lessons as a couple.

23. John 207

Doing volunteer work and helping out an AIDS organization keeps this mother going after her son dies from the disease.

24. Robert 214

A son dies in a helicopter crash and a father learns he can measure his recovery by helping others in crisis.

25. A Final Thought… 221

Part 3: Photos of the Children 223

Part 4: Resources 231

Part 5: Appendix 241

Foreword

As a family therapist, I've had the privilege to work with many parents who experienced the devastating loss of a child. Whether an infant or an adult, the hopelessness that pervades these parents is the same. Their loss does not make any sense to them. It seems to run contrary to nature. Yet, over time and with help, these parents do move forward. They begin a process of defining for themselves how to live a life of hope, purpose and meaning without their child.

Sandy Fox knows this struggle first hand. Because of her willingness to share her story and her adeptness at having others share theirs, she has been able to compile a volume of life stories from families who have been there. In these 25 stories, parents recount their losses with love and encouragement for those who wish to be survivors. Parents show the strength they found to live with what has happened to them.

For parents whose lives have been shattered through the loss of a child, this book will deliver a lifeline of support. Readers will find the stories familiar and the messages enlightening. They will also begin to believe that they, too, can live a meaningful life again. Sometimes it is only through another's experience that we can find the strength in ourselves to move forward. Thank you to these families who were courageous enough to let us see into their souls so that others may learn from them.

Robin Byrne M.S.W.
Carefree, Arizona

Acknowledgements

Many friends and survivors have contributed their stories and feelings to this book. A simple thanks doesn't come near to expressing my appreciation, but here it goes anyway.

Thanks to the many organizations who were so helpful with information and referrals. They include: The Compassionate Friends, Alive Alone, M.A.D.D., S.A.D.D. and Parents of Murdered Children.

For each parent across the United States I spoke to, I can only say from the bottom of my heart, you have touched me in a way I will never forget. Your enthusiasm, your ability to be frank and open with me during our interviews and your kind words after reading the stories I wrote about all of you have created a bond that will not be broken. For privacy sake, I thank you only with first names and locations: Maxine from New City, NY; Celeste from Chandler, AZ; Helene from Chicago, IL; Veronica from Tempe, AZ; Susan from San Jose, CA; Diana from Oak Brook, IL; Karl from Tucson, AZ; Bernadine from Palm Springs, CA; Bonnie from Peoria, AZ; Sally from Las Vegas, NV; Kathy from Temperance, MI; Barbara from Phoenix, AZ; Maryanne from Garden Grove, CA; Lauraine from Pehachapi, CA; Nat from Chestnut Ridge, NY; Wayne and Beverly from Scottsdale, AZ; Floyd from Cumming, GA; Paul and Bridie from North Branford, CT; Joe and Wanda from Rowen, IA; Wayne and Pat from Milford, MI; Nancy from Scottsdale, AZ; Marion from Verona, NJ; Bernie from Louisville, KY; and Sally from Phoenix, AZ.

To all Marcy's friends, I thank you for sharing your thoughts on a very special person. I learned a lot from all of you who so kindly spoke of the time you spent with my daughter and all the fond memories.

Additional thanks:

To Jess, who spoke from the heart about his daughter, his pride and joy.

To all the parents who were kind enough to send, from their personal collection, available photos of their child or children for use in the book.

To agent Nancy Ellis-Bell, owner of the Nancy Ellis Literary Agency in Willits, California, who believed wholeheartedly in me from the beginning.

To Kate, who did the final editing before publication. Your willingness to give your time and effort and especially your comments are appreciated.

To Michael, whose constant editing, comments and encouragement were extremely valuable.

And finally, to all my friends who were so supportive of this project. Each of you holds a special place in my heart, now and always.

Introduction

To lose a child is the most unbearable loss of all.

To keep my child in my heart forever is a goal I will accomplish.

I have no intention of saying good-bye to my daughter. She was always the most important thing in my life. Why should that ever change? I will talk about her, tell her I love her, relive all the good memories and not concentrate on her death. It doesn't hurt as much now, years later. It is a softer grief, hidden in the recesses of my heart. My grief has taken a back seat, but my daughter never will. I will never, never forget she lived and who she was. Talking about her to others for the rest of my life helps. I'll never get over it, but I have gotten through it. I am a survivor, and joy has returned to my life, albeit a different kind of joy with new companionship and caring from a very special person who has reminded me how to love, laugh and enjoy life again.

Nineteen percent of adults in the United States have experienced the death of a child, any age, any cause, to accidents, murder, suicide, drugs, miscarriage and illness, according to a national study done by The Compassionate Friends organization. My daughter, Marcy, was killed in 1994 by a reckless driver. I am part of those statistics.

I have been a journalist my entire life, first as a reporter, followed by freelancing and then teaching journalism in high school for 28 years. When my daughter died, I was teaching, thankfully. The constant work at school kept me busy through those first horrible years. I made sure I had no time to think. I kept working, working, working, because I knew if I stopped, my body and soul would start to ache as if a slow death was overtaking me and there was no way to stop it. It worked for the most part. I survived the initial grieving period.

I was not comfortable going to grief recovery groups as so many have done. I saw it as a crying session for the new loss, and I much preferred to cry on my own. I didn't want to listen to other stories about guilt, family problems, trouble with siblings, all with the same endings…a dead child. I knew it was not for me. Not so for others. No two people grieve a loss alike. Many have found comfort in being with others, particularly in the beginning.

I knew I needed to read whatever I could get my hands on that dealt with grief. After all, I reasoned, reading and writing were my lifeline, and the books would be my grief group. The few books that were available had portions I found very comforting. "Yes," I would say to myself, "this is how I feel now," or, "No, that's not me," moving on to the next book. They all talked about some of the emotions I found myself going through: the shock, the anger, the helplessness, the disbelief, the despair, the what if's, and the final question, "Why me?" It was comforting to know I was not losing my mind when tears would flow for hours, for days, for months. It was refreshing to read that when my child's name was mentioned, my heart would begin beating so fast I could hardly catch my breath; other mothers felt that same anxiety.

Something, though, was missing from all the advice I read. What happened to these parents as time passed? What did they do to survive, to rebuild, to always make sure their child was remembered. To all of us who have lost children, our child is always there with us, in the morning when we rise, as we dress, as we prepare for the day and go about our daily routines, and particularly at night, when the dreams and nightmares visit us. The days roll into weeks, months, years, and most psychologists pronounce us well again. But are we?

Upon retirement I feared grief would be my constant companion. To my great relief I found that not to be true. I knew I needed to channel my grief, my feelings, through the one thing that had been a part of my whole life…writing. My husband and I settled into a new community I immediately came to love, with new friends who were some of the most genuine people I had ever met. Here were people who had never met Marcy, yet wanted to know all about her, see pictures, videos and most importantly, make sure she was always a part of our conversations. I felt a peace and contentment settle over me I had not known since my daughter's death, and I realized I was going to be a survivor.

That was a turning point for me. Everyone grieves differently. Some grieve for shorter periods of time, some longer. I've learned to respect that. One element, though, always remains the same: the pain may lessen, but it never goes away completely. Those who accept this are able to move on. Others find it more difficult.

On the fifth anniversary of my daughter's death, six months after retiring, I felt a great need to write something I believed to be very important for surviving parents. At the time, though, I wasn't quite sure what the approach should be. I wanted the human element I couldn't find in the books I read. I wanted to hear stories of the everyday person, not the famous person, who lived through this devastation and what they had done to move on with their lives, pick up the shattered pieces and become productive human beings. There were no books like that on the market.

I had a goal. What could I write for these individuals having difficulty moving on with their lives to offer them hope? How could I make them understand that at the end of that long road towards healing they could perhaps find a new joy, a new meaning in their life? And how could I give credit to those who had done wonderful things with their lives? I couldn't do it myself, I realized. But others could help me. I began meeting parents who had lost children many years before and now had so many wonderful accomplishments, many honors, much happiness and healing techniques they used in their daily lives. An idea was born, and it wouldn't let go. Have those parents tell their stories of hope and survival along with mine.

What has evolved is a collection of true stories from parents across the country who have lost a child or all their children. It is their story in their own words as told to me, dealing with the emotions and the heartache that lie beneath a broken heart. Only one parent chose to write the entire story, and I just edited it. I spent more than an hour talking to each parent or couple, and by the end of the interview, I knew I was a richer person for having heard their story. It is my hope that the challenges faced by these parents can help those still suffering and acknowledge those who have moved forward. Singer Judy Collins, whose son committed suicide in 1992, said, "There is no one who can help to heal the pain as much as another survivor, sharing his or her story."

In these interviews parents tell the story of their child, what happened and their overwhelming feelings at the time and up to 35 years later. Each story tells of a different type of death and various reactions. All the children were different ages, different backgrounds, different personalities. Parents explain what they have done over the years since their child or children died. Some channeled their grief constructively by doing things as simple as having a building, a location or a scholarship set up in their child's name. Some worked as volunteers. Others had causes. Drunk-driving laws were changed, murderers were kept locked up their entire lives, waiting periods for gun purchases were challenged, parents turned to God and spirituality. Many found it comforting to talk about their child, to have someone listen, even if it had been 5 years, 10 years, 20 years or 35 years later. I understood that feeling and told them so.

All parents acknowledged that they have returned, at their own pace, to the land of the living, and their child will always be remembered. They have no intention of saying good-bye to their child either and will continually tell the child how much they are loved, now and forever. The relationship stays, even though parent and child may not be together physically. These parents focus on the good memories of their child, not the death. And, in doing so, they honor their child.

Many times during the interviews parents broke down. Even if the child died a long time ago, emotions took over, and it was hard for them to speak without tears flowing or voices shaking. Other times parents would laugh at a funny incident involving their child or repeat something the child said that they always remember. Whether I knew the child was not important. I could empathize with all of them no matter the circumstances. Some interviews were so powerful it took me weeks to get back on track and continue writing.

Although all the parents interviewed are different, some commonalities exist: (1) all want to leave memorials of some type to honor their child, (2) all chose to find a cause, a reason to move on with their lives and spoke of how they would live those lives, (3) all believe everyone grieves differently and at different rates, and that as painful as it is, it is important to go through this process to come to terms with the reality of the loss, (4) all of them know they will have setbacks and/or a rush of emotions that can be overwhelming when they might least expect it; it does not mean they will not heal, and (5) all believe they are different people now than they were when their child was alive; they have different goals; different friends; different priorities; and a life with a new richness to it that focuses on what our children left us...the gift of having them.

After each story I provide a brief commentary concentrating on giving some additional information about these people through observations and facts, addressing a problem they have worked out or going into more depth on a grieving issue, and finally, tying it all together. These survivors have learned great compassion and an extraordinary ability to open their arms and hearts to a life without their child.

I realized, in the process of this writing, the entire project was cleansing for me also. I was able to tell my story. It is longer than the others, revealing not only my daughter's life, but my most private thoughts I have never shared with anyone after her death.

My daughter always asked me when I was going to write "the great American novel." I would always smile and say, "Someday." She would then ask, "Will I be in it as one of your characters?" Again, I would smile and say, "Sure, why not?" Never in my wildest imagination did I believe I would be writing an entire book in which my daughter would be my complete inspiration.

It is my wish that through my story and the others, family members, friends, grief therapists, psychologists, those working in hospitals, funeral homes, churches, synagogues, all the wonderful organizations that have helped and, most of all, the brave, grieving parents in the world, will find comfort, hope and to those who need it, the courage to live again.

PART 1

Marcy's Story

To my daughter,

A special place in my heart
Is reserved only for you.
The happiest day of my life-
When you entered it;
The saddest-when you left.
You brought me only joy
Never sadness nor tears.
I carry my love for you with me always.
I was always so proud of you
Your accomplishments, your successes.
Your beauty warmed my heart.
But what surprises me the most
Is what I never knew until recently,
Your inner beauty, your affect on others,
How you touched so many lives.
It is their everlasting feelings for you
That will one day make me whole again.
For they will keep your memory alive
Along with me.
I will never stop loving or remembering you.
Nothing ever dies that is remembered…

Mom
March, 1994

1

Prologue

"The human spirit is stronger than anything that can happen to it."

C.C. Scott

When the phone rings late at night in my Scottsdale home, my mind returns to March 2, 1994, 11:30 p.m. At that moment my life changed forever.

I had fallen asleep around 10:30 p.m., exhausted from a full day's teaching and must have been in a very deep stage of the sleep process when the shrill ringing next to my bed jolted me upright. It took a moment to realize where I was and to focus my mind and eyes.

I let the phone ring once more to be sure it was not the fire or burglar alarm accidentally going off.

"Hello," I said, trying to sound like I had been wide awake as my eyes focused on the clock beside the bed. Inside, the anger boiled. Who would have the nerve to call at such an hour?

"Sandy," said a hoarse but vaguely familiar voice. "It's Pat."

Pat was Simon's mother. My 27-year-old daughter, Marcy, and Simon, at 34 a true English gentleman, had just married five months before in Los Angeles.

"Hi, Pat." Might as well sound friendly, even if the hour didn't appeal to me. Not everyone worked during the week. Maybe she and Basil were just late owls, something I would never be.

"Oh, Sandy, something has happened." I didn't notice the intense anguish in her voice at the time.

Something has happened to Basil, I thought. Recently, he'd had a serious heart operation. Perhaps…a heart attack. Perhaps…he had died suddenly.

"It's the worst thing I could ever tell you," she went on when I didn't respond.

"What's the matter?" I asked. Maybe it wasn't Basil. Maybe something had happened to Simon.

She didn't hesitate, but as she spoke, her voice broke. "Marcy…is dead."

She waited for a response. Her words didn't register. No, that is not possible, I thought. Not my daughter. Why would anything happen to my daughter? In anyone's terms she was the perfect child growing up, never giving me a moment's heartache. My mind refused to accept what she was saying, but I could hear my voice whisper, "What happened?"

"A car accident. I don't know much. The police just called. Something about 7 p.m. this evening. I wondered why Marcy and Simon hadn't come by to pick up the other car. I didn't think anything of it, thought maybe they were too busy at work and would come tomorrow." I quickly interrupted her rambling.

"And Simon?" Why was I even thinking of him? Didn't I hear what this woman had just said. My beautiful daughter was dead. No! It was impossible. No! No! No! I didn't believe it. My heart pushed against my chest as if straining to get out. I took a deep breath to quell the light-headed feeling. I must not faint. There were too many questions my unaccepting mind wanted answers to.

"Simon is alive. They've taken him to Cedar's Sinai Hospital. He's in critical condition. They don't know if he will live or not…5 percent chance, they said. I must go now. I must go to the hospital. I..." Her voice drifted off.

"Wait! Will you call me later, let me know." I needed to talk, to find out more information. What exactly had happened? Where was Marcy? Lying in the wreck, blood covering her body. Why was Pat saying good-bye? Didn't she understand? I continued the deep breathing to stay focused.

"Yes, of course. Are you okay? Should I call anyone? Jess?"

Call anyone? Who was there to call. Jess and I had divorced three years earlier after 27 years of marriage and one child. Sure, he had a right to know, but I should tell him, not Pat. And I'd have to call Michael, my husband at the time, who worked as a teacher in Tucson during the week, 120 miles away. If I called Jess, he could call everyone else, not me. How would I tell him? How would I tell anyone? How did I even know for sure it was true. It could have been a horrendous prank. I'd have to call the police, get the number of the morgue, ask them if they had her body. I had to do that before I could even call Jess. If it wasn't true, it would be a horrible sick trick to play on anyone. Then I would need to make lesson plans and get them to school before morning.

My brain was functioning, it seemed, although my chest felt ripped open and part of my heart torn from my body. I had to concentrate on taking deep breaths so that what was left of my heart could keep me going, at least for the moment. I needed to answer Pat's question. My mind clicked back to the present.

"No, I'll do it," I said, and we disconnected. Don't call Jess yet. First make sure. Could I be dreaming? Was that possible? Or could I just pretend it was three hours earlier when I had called Marcy and left a message on the machine about a great deal I could get her in Hawaii for a June trip. I caught my breath. Had the accident already happened when I had left the message? Was she already dead by then? No, I thought determined. No. I don't even know if all this is true yet. I must call the L.A. police department. See if they did a report on an accident. I dialed information and then long distance. When they answered I explained what I had just been told.

"Yes, yes, there was an accident," said a tired sounding officer. I'm sorry, though. I can't give out any information other than that. No one has been notified."

"Yes they have. I was notified. I was called. Is it true? Is she dead?"

"I'm sorry, but how do I know who you really are."

"What?" Was he kidding? Would I be calling and asking such questions if she were not my daughter? My mind turned over and over. The dizziness was starting to envelop me. And the tightness in my stomach…surely, any second my insides would burst through the skin. Yet, no sound came from my lips.

The officer must have realized how heartless he sounded for in the next second with a kindness and resignation that comes only from those who have done this over and over and not liked it one instant, he said quietly, "Try calling the coroner in South L.A. They can give you the information you're looking for."

"Thank you," I answered just as kindly. How many parents had he called just this week. Quite a few, I was sure. His heart spoke what his voice could not. It was a rotten job for anyone to have.

Unable to make the next move, I sat staring at the wall knowing this one call could turn my world upside down. Before I realized what I was doing, I saw my fingers press the numbers I had written down. Wait, I'm not ready to know. I'll never be ready to know. A woman answered.

"Hello." She waited. "Hello…is anyone there?"

"Hello," I finally managed. "I need to check on an accident…a body…woman…dead." The words would not come in a clear coherent sentence. The word "dead" was not part of my vocabulary where my daughter was concerned. The woman knew exactly what I wanted to know, but it had not been the only accident that night involving a death. Putting me on hold, she said she would check. If she took a long time, I reasoned, that was a good sign. No body, no name. It didn't happen. She was at the hospital with Simon. The woman was back within a minute.

"Yes," she said, "she's here. Marcy Jeanne Lewis is the name?"

I didn't respond. My body froze.

"I'm...so sorry."

"Thank you," I said remembering I should be polite. Clutching the phone tightly to my ear, I lost all sense of movement. My mind reached back to the day 37 years ago when I could hear my mother crying in the next room and screaming my father's name. "He's dead. Oh God, he's dead," I finally heard mom say. I could feel my heart begin to palpitate and my breathing become erratic. I had to urinate very badly.

And then, from the depth of my soul a scream so guttural, more like an animal that had been caught for the kill, worked its way to the top and exploded from my mouth over and over again.

2

The First Hours and Days

"To weep is to make less the depth of grief."

William Shakespeare

After I received the call from Pat, Simon's mom, I sat on the bed staring at the wall, screaming and screaming as loudly as I could. I was alone in the house. I didn't care if I could be heard miles away. This was my only child, the love of my life and now my life was over. Had I been too happy? Was God punishing me for the good life I had had up to this moment? Was I not allowed just a few years of uninterrupted happiness?

My mother had died just two years prior, my dad dead many years earlier; no brothers or sisters on my side or Jess's; no other children; no one left; a few cousins, but they were like strangers. I had lost contact with most of them over the years. What was my reason now for living? Michael, my husband and companion. I had to call him first. I took a deep breath, willed myself to calm down, wiped my eyes, sat at the edge of the bed and reached for the phone. As I dialed his number I rehearsed my apology. "Sorry, my love, for having to wake you up in the middle of the night, but I need to talk to you. I need you."

It rang several times and when Michael picked up I was surprised at how awake he seemed. I recall he never even asked what was wrong, like he was preparing himself for bad news.

"Are you up?" I foolishly asked, my voice still shaking. Is that a way to start a conversation when you're going to tell your husband that your daughter, his stepdaughter, is dead?

"Actually, I couldn't sleep," he said. "I don't know why. What's up?"

Very softly I told him what had happened. The tears began to slide down my face as each word forced its way out of my mouth. His concern for me was evident. He knew what Marcy meant to me, and he, too, felt great love for her in the short time he had known her. He offered to come immediately. I refused to let him drive the two hours in the middle of the night when he was so tired and told him to come when he could in the morning. How could I have even thought he would get any sleep that night. I knew I wouldn't. We hung up.

I waited a while, just sitting there thinking how my world was tumbling down a steep cliff without any way of stopping. I tried to gather the courage to call Jess. I rehearsed what I would say, but nothing seemed right. In the end I just called.

"She's dead," I screamed, when he said he couldn't hear me. "Marcy is dead!" His sharp intake of breath and his "Oh, my God, no!" was so clear, I knew his night of sleep had also ended. He offered to come, but I asked him not to. What could he possibly do to make me feel any better? I preferred being alone with my thoughts and tears. I did ask him to make all the arrangements and to call me in the morning.

Lesson plans. That's what I would do to pass the time. Who knew how long I'd be out of school. Do a few days worth at least. The tears stopped. When I think back now I must have been in deep shock. Breathing was difficult, and I continually found myself in the bathroom urinating. But no more tears just then. It was as though another human being had taken my place and was functioning for me, writing down what needed to be done in my classes.

Before I knew it, a few hours had passed and Michael called again. He had not slept, had already prepared his classes and was on his way to Phoenix. I took a deep breath. It was a good thing he was coming, because now Marcy had been dead for almost six hours, and I could hardly stand the thought of what I would do when I saw the sun come up.

By 6 a.m. I had called my principal, my stepsister-in-law and two dear friends. I knew they would take care of the rest and soon my whole world would know of my sorrow. I didn't really care who knew. In fact I didn't care much about anything. I got in the car, drove to school, left my lesson plans before anyone arrived and walked out, not caring if I ever returned. I still knew nothing about what had happened, and in the car my mind conjured up a series of events leading up to the accident, how she had died, who had tried to save her, if she had said anything at all, what she looked like…

Michael's arrival brought new tears from both of us. In between the phone ringing, the funeral arrangements being made, the air flights confirmed to fly to Los Angeles, canceling engagements for the next few weeks, I stood under the shower, hoping the water could wash away everything that had happened in the last nine hours.

Late that morning when we arrived at Cedar's Sinai Hospital in Los Angeles we found Pat and Basil, Simon's distraught parents, and in intensive care, Simon, barely hanging on to life after a 5 hour brain operation. Pat walked in and out of intensive care every few minutes. She couldn't sit still. Basil, a bit more calm, had contacted the news media, determined to do what he could to catch the person responsible for the accident.

Slowly the story unfolded. After work Marcy and Simon were driving through the Beverly Hills area on their way to dinner. Usually they drove separately, but this particular day was special because they had just bought a new Infiniti and were going out to celebrate. Simon took Marcy to work and picked her up. On Beverly Boulevard in a residential area, a white van going 70 mph missed a stop sign, plowing into the driver's side of the Infiniti. The car was pushed sideways stopping only when it hit a tree. Marcy was on the side that hit the tree, and she died instantly. Simon, thought dead at first, was discovered barely alive and rushed to the hospital. The driver of the van was apparently not injured. He jumped out the smashed front window as the van lay on its side and ran through the neighborhood yards and over the fences. Eyewitnesses gave descriptions of him on the police reports, but he disappeared into thin air. No fingerprints were found, and only beer cans were in the back of the van, nothing else. A large reward was offered for any information, but to this day no one has ever come forward.

Sometime during the afternoon I spoke to the funeral director in Phoenix who asked me if I wanted to see the body. For some reason I had not thought about that or even considered it as an option. I had to make a decision. Jess was standing next to me, so I asked his opinion. I was in no state of mind to think rationally.

"No," said Jess. "I want to remember her as she was, not as she is now."

Yes, that sounded like a wise choice, so I agreed and told the funeral director our decision. It turned out to be a decision years later I would regret. I should have held her one more time no matter how she looked from the accident. I should have told her I loved her.

He then asked us what we wanted her to wear. Why was he asking us this now? Weren't there more important things to think about, to discuss, than clothing. Apparently not. A decision had to be made right then.

Because of my hesitation, he made a suggestion, and I agreed. I thought we were done, but then the bombshell was dropped. There was some complication about releasing the body, and we would have to wait another 24 hours. We did. There was nothing else we could do.

It was decided with no argument from Pat and Basil that Marcy would be buried in Phoenix, since the outcome for Simon was so uncertain. I was relieved she would be near me always.

Three days later more than 300 people, some from as far away as Italy, stood under a beautiful, warm Arizona March sky as we buried Marcy.

3

Simon

"You cannot prevent the birds of sorrow from flying overhead, but you can prevent them from building nests in your hair."

Chinese Proverb

I don't like the word "closure." To use it when dealing with a child's death is unthinkable. I will never have closure. I will never forget. The pain will always be there, deep down, tearing away at every fiber of my being each time I think of the unthinkable. Although time lessens this pain, the hole in my heart will always be there. But I continue on today, just as I did then. What other choice do I have?

After two hospital visits to Los Angeles, I lost all contact with Simon.

When we knew that Simon would live, albeit with some memory limitations after a 5-hour brain operation and a partially paralyzed left side, Michael and I went to Los Angeles to see him a month after the accident. Pat had called and said Simon wanted to see us.

As we walked toward his hospital room, I felt awkward. How should I respond to him? Was it appropriate to cry or should I restrain myself, if possible, and smile, letting him take the initiative? There was so much I longed to ask him about Marcy, about their last day together. I did not know at the time he had no memory of anything that happened that day and might never remember, according to doctors. It had taken him two weeks just to remember he had a wife.

Michael took my hand as we entered the room. Turning toward me with his eyebrows creased together in a question, I knew he felt the tremors running through my body, and I smiled at him awkwardly.

Simon's door was open. He sat propped up in bed, neatly covered to his waist, an anxious look on his face. Pat and Basil flanked both sides of the bed. Everything looked too neat, too controlled, I thought, as we moved toward him with our arms outstretched. I wanted to say, "OK, ready for scene 2, take 3." It was something Simon might have said in production of one of his recent movies.

"Sandy, Michael, I'm so glad you're here." His face bore no scars from the month before. The curly hair had grown in around the scalp and he wore his glasses for better focus. His left eye had no peripheral vision, and, we were told, it might never come back. His voice was warm and gentle as we had always known him to be, but his eyes spoke a different language. As I looked at them, it was as though they were shouting at me. "How could this have happened? How could my life have been destroyed this way? I am dead…dead….dead. Nothing can make it right again." My sentiments exactly, I thought.

His parents left the room to get something to eat (right on cue), and the three of us were alone.

"You look good Simon," I said. He ignored my comment.

"If for one minute I ever thought I was responsible for that accident, I…" Michael and I quickly looked at each other, knowing we had to quell that feeling from him. We didn't let him say another word.

"Of course, you're not," we reassured him, putting our arms around him as he cried quietly. "Everyone knows what happened. Don't ever think that." He calmed down almost immediately. We talked about our cruise we had recently been on and our upcoming vacation, everything except what we really wanted to talk about.

We stayed for an hour that day and returned the next morning before leaving the city. He was more relaxed during our second visit. That original tension was gone. I helped him recall some of their friends, most of whom were still lost in his memory. As I would mention a name, he would crave more information as his eyes would light up with the memory. "Yes," he would say brightly, more than once that day. "Now I remember." I could see that if someone fed him the information, the memory would return. I sensed deep down I couldn't rely on Pat to do that. I would return again soon, I vowed. What I did discover that day was that I could not mention Marcy's name nor did he more than once or twice. Too soon, I thought. Next time we come we'll be able to discuss her.

But it was no different a month later. Simon's memory was returning, the paralysis was definitely retreating, and he looked healthier as we wheeled him around the hospital corridors. But any talk of Marcy was limited to a fleeting sentence about something funny that had happened involving her or a remark she made about one of her friends. At one point, Simon glanced at my right hand and saw Marcy's sapphire ring I always wore (her favorite) which was recovered from the accident scene. At that time it was the only thing I had of hers, and I treasured it. It was always on my finger; I never let it out of my sight. He took my hand, and I glanced at Michael. I didn't want to cause additional stress, so I just waited for his response.

"You know, Marcy used to have a ring just like this one," he said.

He remembered, I thought. That was good, but how should I answer him? "Oh, what a coincidence, Simon. I didn't know," I could say. What a lie that would be, and why should I lie? He would someday have to face the fact that I wore her jewelry, her clothes. It made me feel close to her. She was there with me in everything I did, helping me to make decisions, enjoying 'my' life now that she could not enjoy her own.

"It is Marcy's," I heard myself say and waited for his reaction.

"Oh," was all he said and let my hand go. We realized it would be a long time before Simon would feel comfortable talking about her. We had no idea it would be the last time we would ever have contact with him.

We left for a European vacation the following week, tried hard to enjoy what we could, sent Simon postcards and called upon returning, only to be told by Pat that Simon was now home but not ready to talk to anyone yet. He was in intense and exhausting physical therapy three times a week. She had also kept from him all cards and letters sent to him from me and all of Marcy's friends that wished him a speedy recovery. I called Marcy's friends who were close to Simon and discovered no one had spoken to him those two months we had been gone. In fact, Simon's parents had cut off all contact between Simon and the outside world. We knew nothing of his progress and now, many years later still know nothing. I wrote, I called, but no one responded. I know through one of his friends he was determined to get completely well, to be whole again, before he reentered the outside world. Physical therapy was his world at the time and nothing else mattered. My mind flashed back to the sterile hospital room that first day we saw him, and I remembered thinking how contrived the scene was. Were they all acting then? Are they acting still? I will probably never know.

Why? I kept asking myself. What reason would his parents have to do this to Simon, to me, to Jess, to all their friends? I have discovered over the years there is no answer to this question, only speculation.

Marcy's belongings were finally sent to me two years after her death (I constantly pleaded during that time to get anything of hers I could simply hold, touch, but to no avail.) His parents insisted Simon wasn't ready to deal with it at first nor two years later, but finally relinquished the items. Along with the belongings were hints that nothing was kept by Simon, not one memento, not one picture. Everything was in those 26 boxes, except for a few items belonging to my mother. I had given them to her just a week before the accident, the very last time I saw her.

His parents insisted they could not find anything else. When I looked into her jewelry box, I saw her gold wedding ring. I'm sure it was inadvertently sent, or maybe I am wrong. Maybe all traces of a wife were eliminated by parents who felt they were doing the best for their son. Who knows what they told him, how they convinced him it would be better if he would get on with his life. But to pretend she never existed! How could they! How could anyone do that to another human being?

All these years later, I still have a bitter taste in my mouth about the circumstances surrounding Simon and his recovery. Through it all, though, I am still optimistic that someday he will contact me, that there is a reason for this silence, that he will want to share every bit of Marcy that I could offer him. I know I would like to have his thoughts and feelings of her time with Simon, probably the happiest of her life. Not one friend or family member shares my optimism.

I am thankful that Marcy does not know how this has all turned out. She would be sad to learn that the Simon she knew may no longer exist. I am sad for Simon, myself and every one of Marcy's friends who loved him so much. But I must wish him well, for my own well-being, rather than drown in resentment of what could have been.

4

The Background Years

"Wherever you are, I am there also."

Beethoven

Someone once asked me, "What was the happiest moment in your life?" I didn't hesitate for a minute. I just smiled and said, "The day my daughter, Marcy, was born, July 27, 1966." It was the most private, personal moment of my life. Nobody but the doctors were with me in that operating room where I had to have a caesarean section, and selfishly, I wanted it that way. I had carried her for eight months, and it was truly my moment of glory. The feeling was triumphant, as though I had just won the mother of the year award for producing the most beautiful, perfect baby that ever existed. (But doesn't every mother feel that way?) I had made a new life. She had grown inside only me. No one else, even my husband at the time, could feel the exhilaration, the ecstasy, the fascination I was feeling knowing that this human being was a part of me.

When I finally saw her the next day, her bright black eyes looked into mine, and I fell in love. She was beautiful, and it surprised me completely. My looks were just "ok", my husband's, just "ok", but here was this beautiful creature, head filled with jet black hair and tiny hands and feet like a baby doll. Looking at her hair I laughed to myself, "No wonder I had such heartburn all the time, with that load of hair!"

I remember the proud nurse saying as she busily straightened my sheets the first morning, "Wait till you see the birth picture we took. It should turn out great. She was fast asleep, so we combed her hair and poked her. Her eyes flew open and the camera clicked. Should turn out great, she repeated." I smiled, dreamily thinking, how could it not.

The first few years of Marcy's life, fear constantly gripped me about whether I was an adequate mother. Maybe it was guilt. I had gone back to school to get my master's degree and at 12 months started putting her in a nursery school for the mornings so that I could attend classes. My few close friends looked at me like I was completely out of my mind. Their words vibrated in my head constantly. "Leaving your daughter so young." "How do you know she's getting good care." "So much sickness, she's bound to always have a runny nose." "Is education that important you'd risk something happening to her at the nursery." "Stay at home like a normal mother would." And the looks. Disgust at my choices. The whispering behind my back. In the sixties if you had a child, you didn't work, you didn't have a career. Motherhood was paramount.

All concerns proved unfounded. I soon discovered Marcy thrived with the companionship of little ones her age and older. She talked, she walked, she was potty trained by 15 months. And she was the darling of the nursery school. Everyone loved her from the teachers to the other children, to the owner. They raved at how smart she was, how quick to learn, how so very pretty with her long brown hair pulled back in a ponytail and how neat she always looked. Perhaps that was the start of what turned out to be a thriving childhood, full of adventures and misadventures, winning and losing friends, loneliness at times and her constant asking me if she would ever have a sister or brother.

In a way those women of the sixties were right. I did miss out on a lot I'm sure. I started teaching when she was four. Her father was busy pursuing a career as a stockbroker and paid little attention to her during the weekdays. Her grandmother did most of the taking, picking up and babysitting of Marcy throughout her young life. I comforted myself by saying to everyone, "Look at all the fantastic experiences she is able to have being with so many different people and getting along with them all." The truth was that I was desperately trying to convince myself that it was okay to be a part-time mother.

Again, though, Marcy thrived. Perhaps it was what made her what she was at the time of her death and perhaps because of my own busy life, it is the reason I never knew how others saw her until I received the notes and letters.

Those first few years I thought she was the prettiest of all my friends' kids. Her big brown eyes, short pug nose and bright smile could light up any room full of children. One year I decided to enter her in a beauty pageant for those under four years old. Her light brown hair was all the way down her back, so I would put it in a ponytail with front bangs and was sure it was the cutest look going. She hated dresses, so most of the clothes she wore were matching pants and tops. When I dressed her for the interview to be done on a large school auditorium stage, there were no ringlets or curly hair, no lacy dress with patent leather shoes. She wore a pantsuit, her hair pulled back as she usually wore it. It was a Marcy look. The wait was interminable. I did whatever necessary to keep her from getting cranky before the interview. Other young children began crying or whining, and mothers looked embarrassed. Marcy just watched quietly, taking it all in. Finally, her turn came. With a dry sense of humor I remember her interview was far from serious. She had the audience laughing during the entire three minutes she was on stage. In the end it was the frilly dress and ringlets that won. Marcy didn't seem to care. She had had fun on that stage (a sign of what was to come in high school). For me, I was disappointed, but two mothers who I didn't even know boosted my spirits when they came up to me afterward in the audience and said, "Your daughter should have won. She had the most personality!" "Thank you," I smiled to them and then all the way home. For me it was victory enough.

Marcy was far from perfect (as much as a mother hates to admit it). In those years while she was in elementary school I saw the stubbornness that could flare up if she didn't get her way. When she did something her father or I didn't approve of, she was not hit; she was punished by being sent to her room where she was to stay until she acknowledged her wrong doing. Sometimes she would dramatically cry and move closer to our room so we'd be sure to hear her. "She must have learned that in drama," I would whisper to her father and smile. If she heard me, she would cry even louder. Finally, when she knew it was fruitless to continue her temper tantrum, she would come out of her room as if nothing had happened and talk to us about the most mundane daily occurrences.

I also saw the perfection in everything she did, at nursery school, in elementary school and in high school, sometimes to extreme. Everything always had to be neat, whether it be her room, her report for science or her reign as president of a youth group. A good student who got excellent grades, she hid the frustration of never quite being the one chosen for the drama play part she so desperately wanted, of never quite being the most popular kid in the class, of never winning first place in a school speech contest. Instead of letting it get her down, she settled for what she could do. She worked behind the scenes for every high school play. She was the makeup artist, the one who put together the scenery or props or the operator of sound and lights. She was active in speech tournaments, toured with the debate team and sometimes even came home with minor awards and ribbons. The award certificates piled up, and I framed every one of them and put them on her wall. Not being very active in sports she was always the last one chosen for a team. (Her coordination was not the best.) She was friendly to those who would never have given her the time of day and tried to fit in as best she could.

Eventually, she became wise enough to just relish the good friends she had made through elementary, high school and in youth groups.

She learned the hard way, as most children do, that kids can be cruel. She made sure she was always there for the underdog, the one who sat in the corner alone and the one who had a handicap others made fun of. She complimented them on what they could do and would invite them over to the house.

"Mom, you're such a fast typist, please type my term paper." From junior high through high school, this was just one of my roles. If it wasn't done to her satisfaction, I would find myself up late into the night. To ease my load at age 16, we got her a car. There were too many parties, too many clubs, too many after school events. I used to tell friends that I would have given her a car at 14 if the law had allowed it! She was responsible enough, and I trusted her completely.

As my friends agonized over their teens who had gotten out of control with trying drugs and drinking in the 70's and 80's, that was something I never had to worry about. Somehow we had instilled in her a moral code she did not find reprehensible as did others her age who lashed out at their parents by dying their hair pink, wearing outrageous clothing or by going out with someone at least 10 years older. In fact, the group she hung around with always seemed to be from good families with good values, and it was just one less thing I had to worry about as she grew up.

"God," I would say to myself, "am I lucky. What did I ever do to deserve such a great kid?" I anguished with other mothers as their kids ran away from home, stayed out all night or shoplifted at the local Walgreens. But it was hard for me to relate to their problems.

Boys came along in the teen years and Marcy was pleased there were a few that even liked her enough to take her out. As always she was very particular. They didn't have to be extremely handsome, but a good person inside. I was always confident she knew the difference. When a very good looking one did come along for a few months and then moved on, her blood pressure would go up, her nose would start to bleed, and tears would flood her face, while her friends and I tried comforting her as we wiped away the tears.

When, finally, a permanent boyfriend arrived on the scene at 16, a change came over Marcy that seemed to follow her for the rest of her life. She gained a confidence about herself that propelled her to new heights. Friends were always in the house. She was always going out with the girls or in groups of girls and boys to concerts, to parties, to dances. She didn't feel the need to go searching for that Mr. Right. He was by her side those years and throughout college. Although she became frustrated with his lack of ambition at times, she said she would follow him to the other side of the country, which she came within a hair of doing. I swore it was her life, and I wouldn't be an interfering mother. I still have a thank you card she sent me for accepting what she was going to do after graduation and not trying to change her mind. It said, "You're the greatest, Mom. Thanks for letting me make my own mistakes."

As sometimes happens, in growing up you find that what **you** want is just as important as what your boyfriend wants, and so upon graduating from Arizona State University, she boldly announced she was heading to California, with or without him. She wanted a career in advertising, and that was the place to start. He followed her, but as things have a way of happening, they eventually broke up, and Marcy met the love of her life, Simon, who at the time, had a law degree but was heavy into film producing in Hollywood and teaching the techniques at the University of Southern California part-time. She landed a wonderful job at the L.A. Music Center as the marketing director and began her whirlwind life in the company of the famous theater people she had envied in high school. But this time she was on the side of the fence she wanted to be on. Parties, meeting people, out almost every night, she began leading a life she had only dreamed about.

I knew Marcy had made many new friends in her Los Angeles life, but living 400 miles away in Phoenix, it was hard to access those people as I had done when she was younger. I knew she was happy. When I would visit, she would introduce me to some of her friends, and there wasn't one person I didn't think was fabulous.

When her roommate, through a quirk of fate, won $1 million in a VISA charge contest, she was intensely happy for her. "Tell me," I said one day, "Aren't you a tiny bit jealous that it wasn't you who charged that lamp the two of you bought?" Without a moment's hesitation she said, "Oh no, I'm really happy for her," and changed subjects immediately. I could see she meant it. I know if the shoe had been on the other foot, I would have been extremely jealous and mostly irritated that I had allowed my friend to charge the lamp on her own VISA, when it was my lamp! Wisely enough, Marcy knew that the money was not important. "Look, Mom, she really needs the money. I'm doing just fine." I realized the friendship was more important to her than any amount of money. I admired her tremendously at that moment and was very proud of her.

Marcy married Simon on a beautiful fall day, October 10, 1993. She planned the wedding entirely without my help but with the help of some friends. I had a Phoenix engagement party for her and two showers were held in Los Angeles, one of which I had the pleasure of attending. Up to the last minute before the wedding Marcy was her organized self, calling the caterer, the florist, the bakery, the musicians and the hotel 24 hours prior to the affair, making sure all was in order. She wanted the day to be perfect and it was. A three week honeymoon in Greece followed before their normal life resumed.

I talked to Marcy once or twice a week during the next few months. She was very happy, making plans to purchase a home. Then she and Simon would talk about children. Lynn, her best friend, got married four months after Marcy and keeping Lynn organized through the shower in Phoenix and eventually the wedding kept her quite busy and involved in Lynn's life.

The day after Lynn and Marc's wedding was the last time I ever saw her. Ironically, I had to take her and Simon to the airport to fly back to Los Angeles because her sister-in-law's father had died, and she wanted to attend the funeral. It is good to know that the last time I ever touched her was with a great big hug and kiss when she left my car. I can still visualize her waving goodbye.

Her happiness and mine were short-lived. The following week she was dead, Simon barely alive, and the driver of the van was never held accountable.

5

Private Thoughts on Healing

"What we have once enjoyed deeply we can never lose. All that we love deeply becomes a part of us."

Helen Keller

A DIFFERENT LIFE

When your child dies, you change. The person you were before is gone. The life you had before is no longer possible. You rebuild, with different expectations, with different responses. You learn to have fun again, albeit, in a different way. You learn it is okay to grieve whenever and wherever you want and not to feel ashamed of your feelings. You know your heart will always be broken, but you are a survivor...for now anyway.

The littlest things become important. Pausing to gaze at a beautiful fiery sunset can bring tears to my eyes. The earth is so beautiful and my daughter will no longer see any of that beauty or live the life she so enthusiastically was building for herself and her husband. I understand now, as I watch the yellow hues turn to pink and orange, then yellow, and finally a misty blue as night falls, how everything around me can change in a split second. In one second I had an energetic, enthusiastic daughter eager to tackle life's ups and downs; the next second she lay lifeless in a pile of carnage too unbearable to even think of.

As each day brings a new sunset, my life changes too. My compassion for others has deepened. As I watch the news every evening and hear of children who are hungry, need medical attention or are caught in a war zone with no where to turn and no one to help, my eyes fill with tears and I want to reach out to them. Or hearing of a shooting at a school and how many children have died, I want to pick up a phone and call those suffering parents. I know how they feel. It is a feeling no one who has not gone through this could possibly ever understand. Others can empathize with you, but they do not, nor ever could, understand the feelings you have suffered and will always suffer for the rest of your life. The pain subsides with time. It gets a little better as the years go on, but it never goes away completely. You are always left with an emptiness in your heart and mind of what could have been, what should have been.

It is useless to ask "Why?" or speculate on "What if's?" I want to slap the person who says to me as they hold my hand, "She is in a better place now." Don't preach your religious beliefs to me! She is not in a better place. Here on earth was the best place...with me...with Simon...with everyone who loved her. I have always, however, held the philosophy that everything has a reason for happening and in many circumstances it has kept me going after a sickness, a death, an accident. But this...this child's death, could not possibly have a reason. Is God that cruel that he takes from us the thing we love most at the worst time, in the worst way? This can't be happening. This happens to other people, not me. I know my broken heart will never heal, but that I am a survivor and, to my surprise at times, can endure most anything. The worst has already happened. Nothing else can ever be as bad.

Sometimes my eyes fill with tears as I say over and over how unfair this all is. If I could change places with her? Of course, I would. I don't want to die, but neither did she. She had so much more she wanted to accomplish. A family was so important to her. Having children. "I will never have just one child, Mom," she once said. "It is so lonely." I knew the feeling. I was an only child too and wanted desperately to have more than one. It was not in the cards.

BODY LANGUAGE

A few months after the accident, Michael and I were on a train in England, facing each other. I was staring out the window thinking about Marcy, as I did in those first years every waking moment, when I sensed him looking at me.

"You're thinking you would have died in her place if given the chance, aren't you?" he asked.

My profound sense of awe showed on my face. "How could you, out of the millions of things I could have been thinking, have known that?" I asked.

"A hunch, and the expression on your face."

I smiled at him and shook my head in amazement.

I always remember that moment and realize our thoughts are not always private. Our emotions and body language give us away. How many others close to us, I wonder, understand the hell we go through for the rest of our lives?

TIME

When someone talks about an important year in their lives or a news show on TV asks what you were doing when....I always think of Marcy's life. How old was she in 1972? What were we doing then? Years become important in your memory. The year 1966 when she was born, the most important. What was happening in the world then? Viet Nam. President Johnson. The Beatles. A friend says, "Do you remember when we…" "What year was that?" I ask. "Oh, yes, I remember that year." But to myself I associate every year between 1966-1994 with Marcy and what she was about then. If the year is before 1966, it is "before Marcy was born." If the year is 1996, yes, that was an important year, but not that important for me because Marcy was already dead two years by then.

Time has a way of passing very quickly and we lose track of it. I remember when it was the fourth anniversary of Marcy's death, I wondered how that could be. As far as I was concerned, it had all happened just yesterday…no, today. Today, I felt her body hugging mine as we said goodbye at the airport. I could never guess it would be the last time I would ever touch her.

OTHERS' REACTIONS

For months after Marcy died we received beautiful letters, notes and cards telling us how much she was loved by others and what she meant to them. I knew that after a while the messages would stop, but I wasn't prepared for the abrupt ending when it came. One day I walked to the mailbox and nothing was in it. I became very frightened at that moment. It's over. Everyone has gone back to their daily routine, and I am expected to do the same. Those letters were comforting. I didn't realize until that moment how they had kept me going, how I looked forward to hearing from these people who knew her so well. I lost it then. Tears consumed me because I knew the compassion from others was over, and I had to deal with the reality of what I was going to do with the rest of my life.

It was surprising to me how unconcerned and indifferent my co-workers were when I eventually went back to work. It wasn't them that this had happened to.They expected me to mourn and then get on with the rest of my life. I did not blame them for that, and I wasn't angry with them. But what life exactly were they thinking of? Didn't they realize I didn't care about anything except my daughter? Didn't they realize this was an inconsolable loss that no one should ever have to go through? It took me years to reconcile myself with the fact that only those who have gone through this understand any of it, and I could not be angry at others.

THE FRONT

I put on a good front. It is true that work was a salvation of sorts. It kept me busy; it kept me thinking about anything and everything except what I really wanted to think about…Marcy. My mind was focused on teaching while my heart was trying to beat regularly. People would look at me and think, "She looks fine. No need to worry about her. Next problem…."

When I would get home in the late afternoon is when it would all come undone. I was then allowed the freedom to become myself. And what was I? Who was I? Just a shell of a person that for the second time in two years had to deal with a death in the family. Family…what a strange word now. I had none. My dad, dead when I was 13; my mom, dead two years previous to Marcy; and now the unspeakable, my only child, taken from me in the time it takes to see one lightning flash, hear one crash of the cymbals, taste a sour lemon. My husband, Michael, never having any children in a previous marriage could empathize, but never truly understand because it had never happened to him. He had said so himself to me once.

NIGHTMARES

Sometimes I think dark thoughts. She is in that wood box six feet below the surface, shouting to get out. "No, I shouldn't be in here," she says. "Somebody help me." Those and other nightmares haunt me. Sometimes I dream she is alive and we are having a wonderful time in Los Angeles looking for a house for her and Simon. One time she was a small child of five again, and I had a baby sister for her to play with and take care of. Her eyes opened wide, and she smiled as I placed the baby in her arms. Another time she slips from my grip on the edge of a mountain and tumbles into a fathomless bottom. I am jolted awake, feeling my heart palpitating and the sweat on my forehead. In still another dream I lifted the lid of the coffin and saw only skeletal remains. I thought I would see her body sleeping peacefully, but her body was gone. That has been one of the most inconceivable thoughts…that everything she was is no more…in any form.

WE ARE ONE

I do not believe in an afterlife, but I must confess an experience that happened to me a few months after Marcy died has given me pause to believe in the transfer of a person's soul to another live human being. I noticed a weight gain a few months following her death and didn't think too much of it. (She had weighed about 10 pounds more than I.) The one part of my body that had always been small, my breasts, were growing also! I was 50 years old and my breasts were finally a decent size! It took a while to make the connection, and when I did, it was like a bolt of lightning had cleared my head. I believe part of her is now in me. When I look in the mirror, it is her body I see, her curves. I hear myself saying things she once said. I hear my humor mimicking hers. Her friend, Lynn, occasionally tells me in a comment I may make, "You sounded just like Marcy right then. She used to say that." "Really?" I ask.

"Yes," is the soft answer I hear from a woman longing to speak to her best friend again. I wear some of Marcy's clothes occasionally, jackets and sweat shirts that never seem to get old or worn out. I always wear her jewelry. The ring on my right hand was her favorite, seven sapphires inlaid in a straight line of gold. The sapphires were from a cocktail ring of my mother's she had been given, and I am determined it will never come off. It is especially sentimental because my mother is also there with me. Marcy and I are close, we are one when I am surrounded by her and the things she loved the most.

LYNN

Lynn and her family are one of the things she loved the most. I have always loved Lynn like a daughter and knew she and Marcy, who met when they were 14 years old, had a special bond that only two sisters could have. They didn't have to talk to each other every day or every week. Knowing they were there for each other was enough. I often envied their relationship, knowing meaningful relationships like that are hard to come by in a lifetime. Lynn, like many others, was crushed and probably always will be by her death. One moment a few years after Marcy died that made me realize the special relationship they had was when Lynn said, "I met some women my age recently that I feel comfortable with, that can finally fill 'some' of the void left by Marcy's death." I had no idea she had been that lonely those first years. I was happy for her. I knew she would always love Marcy, but no one at that age should have to suffer that much.

One of the happiest moments of my "new" life after Marcy's death was when Marc and Lynn's son Jonah was born, and she asked me to be the godmother. It was the next best thing to being a grandmother, something I could never even hope for. As Jonah grows, his mischievous smile and laughter warm my heart, and I feel a bonding start. I know

Jonah will always be an important part of my life and that we will be close. I think of taking him to the zoo, reading stories to him and watching him grow. How can I help but think of Marcy and how much she and Lynn looked forward to having their children grow up together, to grow old together, to travel and fulfill all the dreams they talked about as teenagers. I sense Lynn thinks about it often, too, although we do not speak of it.

CEMETERY

Because of who I am and who Marcy was, I visit her grave every 2-3 months and especially on her birthday and the day she died. Sometimes there are colorful bouquets of carnations and daisies sitting on top of the grave on March 2 and July 27. There is no card, only a tag saying where they are from. I called the florist one time and was told only that they were from Sherman Oaks, California. No name. I smile, albeit sadly. That is where Simon lives. The first thing I do at the cemetery is wash the stone down and scrape the marble that has her picture embedded in it with a razor blade until it sparkles in the sun and she looks full of life. It is probably the cleanest stone in the cemetery, but I want it that way, and I know Marcy does too. She was a neat-nut like me, and I have a feeling she would expect me to do it. In the back of my mind I also want it to look good for anyone who may come to visit. I then put white silk lilies, her favorite flower, into the ground around the stone. Looking around the cemetery, as I stand there so often, it is obvious that no one takes care of the stones as I do. Most of them look old, worn and have muddy remnants of a recent rain accumulated. One gets the feeling of a deserted war zone many years later. I talk to Marcy. I tell her anything and everything that she would love to know, as though we were having our weekly (or sometimes more often) phone conversations between Phoenix and Los Angeles. I chuckle and can hear her voice laughing with me. Then I gaze into her eyes, time stops and the tears flow. How could she not be sharing this with me? I become angry. At times I am angry at life itself and what it has forced me and thousands like me to endure. I am angry that Marcy was not allowed to accomplish all her goals. I am angry that there is no child, nothing to carry on my family line. I find it hard to stay too long, lest the anger engulf me, so I say goodbye for now.

HOLIDAYS

Holidays are a very difficult time, especially Thanksgiving. It was the last holiday that we were all together as a family and when that time of year comes around, invitations come our way. We go, because not to go is to acknowledge our grief, and I want my grief to be private now. Stories about marriages, laughter at someone who recently divorced or won an honor, all abound at the dinner table from relatives and the children. But my mind is not there. My mind focuses on how Marcy can't enjoy this, how she would love to be here chatting with her cousins and their children, telling her own stories about successes or failures she has had. Some talk about grandchildren. Others keep silent, knowing the effect the word "grandchildren" has on me. The atmosphere is casual, but a tenseness pervades the room because everyone believes they have to tiptoe around many subjects because it may be too painful for me to hear them talk about events that Marcy was once a part of. Her name is rarely mentioned out of what others feel is consideration for the grieving parents.

But they don't understand, and they need to. I want to talk about her, and I want them to talk about her. She will always be alive to me, and I want to keep her memory alive for others. They are all afraid, though. I explain, to the relief of most friends and relatives, how important it is for me to have them talk about her. She will always be a part of my life, and if I can only enjoy the memories, I will at least have that. They breathe a sigh of relief and the once tense atmosphere is now clear.

STRANGERS

When I meet someone new, one of the first questions that is asked after questions about your marital status is "Do you have any children?" How do I answer that? Michael always looks at me and lets me answer. I take a deep breath and say, "I have one child who was killed in a car accident a few years ago." "Oh, I'm so sorry," they say awkwardly but with genuine warmth. The conversation is stalled until I say, "Please don't feel badly for bringing it up." It's a natural question, and I want people to know and understand where I am coming from, that I am acknowledging the proudest accomplishment of my life. If I say, no, I have no children, then am I saying she never existed? In my eyes I am. I want people to know that she not only existed, but was a beautiful human being I am immensely proud of now and always.

HAWAII

One of the special places I think of Marcy is in Hawaii. Oh, how she loved it there, the pristine beaches to lie on, running free in the sand and water. "Mom, look at the shell I found," she would shout enthusiastically to me as she ran up the beach to where I sat smiling at her. "This is the best one in my whole collection!" I pick up shells now as I walk on the beach thinking of a younger Marcy, those tiny bikinis that looked so great on her slim but perfectly curved body. I envied her young figure. A woman in her twenties walks toward me, a beagle at her side. The overwhelming sensation of thinking it is Marcy with her dog Gain, her short brown hair bouncing in the sunlight, her laughter at the dog chasing a crab running up the beach as the waves rush to shore, makes me stop short and close my eyes. Emotions overwhelm me, and when I finally open them again, the woman and dog have both disappeared. They are but a brief reminder of another life, another time, one tucked far down into my heart forever. I continue to walk, continue to breathe, continue to live.

NEW LAWS FOR DRIVERS

A front page article in the Los Angeles Times on May 1, 1994, told of Marcy's accident and a quirk in the car registration law that allows so many people to slip through the system. One of the reasons the man who crashed into Marcy and Simon's car could never be found was because the van was never re-registered after it was purchased from a gentleman in Seal Beach three weeks earlier. The purchaser supposedly bought the white van for $200 and gave a false name and a false address to the original owner so that when the police tried to find the driver, it was a dead end. Many Californians and those who come over the border illegally never bother registering a car, getting insurance or getting a license. Needless to say, because of this, many die unnecessarily. Statistics show that California leads the nation in hit and run traffic accidents, with Los Angeles County accounting for the lion's share. Over half are never caught. The Department of Motor Vehicles estimates that 10 percent of the state's drivers or about two million people drive without a license. LAPD's South Traffic Division says that 65 percent of felony traffic suspects are in the country illegally. They take their chances. It costs them nothing. It cost me everything. Stricter laws need to be put in place, and I hope this will one day come to pass so that more lives can be saved, not destroyed.

MY PRAYER

I now know what real tragedy is. I understand the unbearable pain and that it will always be with me. I understand how people react to you and your pain. I am comforted from those who remember Marcy each day, each month, each year...friends of mine, friends of Marcy's. They are not afraid to mention her name. I have made them feel comfortable knowing I want them to always be a part of my life. Notes, letters and thoughts are always appreciated from those far away, and I answer all of them. I try to live life to the fullest one day at a time. I know now it is okay to laugh when I feel it appropriate and to cry whenever appropriate. I no longer feel as though I am betraying Marcy's memory when I have a good day full of laughter shared with friends and family. In the shadow of my loss, I know I am not alone in my pain. This gives me the strength and courage to forge ahead.

As I open a drawer in my bedroom where I keep some charred remains of the broken headlight I picked up at the scene of the accident, I find comfort in knowing these remains do not describe my life anymore.

6

Personal Thoughts from Marcy's Father, Jess

"Life breaks everyone, but some people grow strong at the breaking places..."

Ernest Hemingway

I couldn't cry. It wasn't real. For two days I was just numb. I functioned, made all the funeral arrangements, was doing what I needed to do next, but all while in a stupor. It was not until I went to Marcy's old apartment where all her friends had gathered two days later and put my arms around Lynn, her best friend, did the release come. Then I cried and cried. Still today, when alone in my car driving or talking to anyone who knew her, my eyes fill with tears.

I think I can trace my emotional response back to my father. My father never showed any emotions. I always saw him as successful; he was in control of his life. The soft part of him was locked deep down. In my effort to be successful, I always tried to be like him. If you weren't supposed to cry, then I would be like that too.

Perhaps that is how I got through the funeral and the eulogy I gave to all the people there. I only cried at the end of the funeral when Sandy, Marcy's mom, and I hugged each other and, through the tears, found it difficult to let go.

A distant relative sent me a letter the following week saying he never writes notes or letters but felt compelled to just then. He said, "What you did at your daughter's funeral was the most courageous thing I have ever seen anyone do. Knowing how important my daughter is to me, it is something I'm sure I could never do. You are truly an inspiration, and Marcy could have never asked for a greater father than you. She was truly blessed!. I shall never forget what I saw you do. You have already made me a better "Daddy" to my daughter."

About a month after the accident I was at a Passover dinner of a friend. Everyone got to talk about the previous year's happenings. This gave me an opportunity to talk and cry about Marcy in a public place. I found it very healing. I was able to share with those I knew and those I didn't know so well. I was told by others that they admired me so much because they could never reveal themselves to another person as I had. One person said, "You have put into words all your feelings. That is healthy. Be patient, but realize the pain never goes away." To this day, when I am asked to give a speech to a toastmaster's group or political gathering, I always include a "Marcy story" about a funny incident or something clever she said. That way she is always with me in good memories.

Since Marcy's death I have a harder time focusing on tasks. I can't concentrate for a long period of time. Something happened to me in the process of her death. I went to a twice monthly grief group at CASA, part of a Franciscan Renewal Center, and there learned I was not crazy. What was happening to me was natural. It was very therapeutic. Others talked about how they couldn't do something they've always done before the death of their child, like balance a check book. The skill was gone. One executive, who carried a list of 20 most important "to do" things every day with him and accomplished all the tasks, found that after his child died, he had trouble completing even one or two things on the list he made each morning. He felt like a failure. Finally, one morning he got up to do his list and put only one thing on it. When he could do that one thing (for example, make toast for breakfast), he then began to put two things on his list each morning. It took him several years before he was up to "five" things, but as his list grew he knew he would survive. Concentrating on a task and completing it is still hard for me to this day, but I know as the days, months, years progress, so do I.

The facilitator for the group said there is no specific length of time to be grief stricken. Americans have the shortest time limit for grieving, he said. In other countries employers give more time to those who need it. I often wonder if I was an employee and it took me two years to recover, would my employer have given me that time or fired me? Answering my own question, I have to say as the employer, I probably would have fired me!

Fortunately, I had my own business at the time of Marcy's death. I gave myself three days and on the fourth day drove to the office, got out, walked to the door, but got no further. I turned around and left. I didn't work a full day for many months. I couldn't work. I didn't want to do it. For what? Everything pleasurable about getting old was gone. My child, who I was very proud of, would no longer be able to do successful things. And I would no longer get the pleasure of her excitement about making sure the ice cream didn't melt when she served 25,000 people at one of her Music Center functions or as she talked about meeting Charlton Heston. Her vigor and excitement added so much to my life, and I would never have that again. Whether I was able to show Marcy my feelings, I don't know. I loved her so much, and although I sometimes frustrated and annoyed her with my ways, such as taking days to return her phone calls, I'm sure she knew how I felt about her. I will always wonder what Marcy wanted when she phoned the day before the accident. I'll never know. I never returned the call.

What bothered me at CASA was when those in the group said my issue was worse than theirs. I didn't believe that. Everyone's issues were important. I didn't want to be the center of attention, so I eventually left. I got what I needed—I wasn't crazy, I wasn't losing my mind, and I knew it would simply work itself out over time.

I also got involved with Mothers Against Gangs, Inc. when I was asked to help them with their accounting books. The group was started to provide support for parents whose children died through violence. In addition to accounting work, I helped them revamp their organizational structure and gave them money. I walked away after a year feeling very good about it.

I always considered myself lucky and even though some bad things may have happened to me, something good always came out of it. Here is something there is no recovering from. I'm lucky that I now have a new, caring family from my second marriage. My wife's grandchildren call me 'grandpa' and it sounds good, feels good and I love them. They fill the void a little, but they are not a part of me. I can have the pleasure a mentor gets, but not the pleasure a father gets. They can't ever take Marcy's place, and that makes me sad. When the 6-year-old asks, "Grandpa, do you have any children?" I answer, "I had a child. She died." The concept is still hard for them at that age and even for someone at my age.

Part of my continual anger stems from Marcy's husband's parents. I wonder how Simon's parents can cut off all communication between Sandy, me and Simon. It is a closure issue with me. In my heart I know even if I was able to see him, over the years I would probably see him less and less because there were no grandchildren, and he would move on with his life. But I loved him. He was a nice guy. I don't blame him for what happened; it was not his fault. I would have liked to spend time with him during all these years, tell him I love him just as much now as before, walk around the block with him, go to the zoo...simple everyday things. Just talking to him would help the healing, but until now there has been no word from him and nothing from his parents telling us how he is doing.

The heartache that comes when the natural order of things is changed, when your child dies before you, is unfathomable. I remember going to the funeral of a friend who died too young and his mother standing over his grave softly yelling at him, "How could you do this to me? I was supposed to die before you, not you before me!" Now when I hear news about a child who dies after being shot, from an illness or in a car accident, I cry. I cry for the child, but I also cry for the parents who are left behind to live with this tragedy for the rest of their lives.

Friends say they see more light and laughter in me now after almost seven years. I smile because they care. But I know they'll never understand how my heart will always ache for Marcy.

Jess's eulogy at Marcy's funeral

Marcy! Sandy and I brought you into the world. We gave you our love and shared our ideas of the world and how it worked with you.

What you did for us is show us that what we told you worked!

You showed us that hard work, focus, organization and desire worked. You showed us that loving, caring, sharing and genuine desire to help others worked.

You seemed to be able to tell the difference between what we said and what we did and were able to choose to do as we said and not as we did.

You had a sense of balance that for me was astounding. Not balance in terms of standing (falling down and walking into walls was something you did well also), but of understanding the people you brought together for projects and meetings. You created or joined many different extended families that are represented here now.

These people work together because you provided the glue that binds them as one.

Marcy, this last year you brought great happiness to your mother and father. Simon met all my requirements for a son-in-law (friends have told me he exceeds even my wish list for you). Your happiness was so very apparent each time we spoke to or saw you. It brought us both great joy.

Marcy, as your parents, we wish we could kiss your hurts, put a bandage on them and make them well, but we can't.

What we can do is tell you that you did darn well and left monuments, that we are very proud to have been part of your creation and your good works, and we know that as you depart into what for us is a place of mystery, that you will excel. We send you off on your journey with all our love.

7

Building Memorials

"To live in hearts we leave behind is not to die."

Thomas Campbell

"She was always supportive and encouraging."

"She brought so many people together."

"She touched our hearts and will never be forgotten."

"I felt lucky she crossed my path."

"Her humor and the importance of friendship."

"She was the organizer, the leader, the glue."

"I always sought her opinion and judgment."

"She had many friends and the ability to put people together."

"She had the gift of gab."

"She added a smile to my day."

"Her advice was always on the mark."

"She was true, genuine, magnificently sincere and so real."

"Her positive attitude brightened our day."

Are they talking about my daughter? What shocks me most is that none of these people who wrote me for months after her death knew the other, so it had to be the truth. The same words repeated over and over: "glued us together, sense of humor, sincere, felt lucky she was my friend." Could it be that I never knew her inner strengths and that this would keep her memory alive for me and so many others? I had to think back through her life. It must have been there all along, as she was growing up and somehow, even though I knew she was a great kid, it had somehow eluded me.

From the more than 500 notes and letters I received, the following are some of the ones I hold close to my heart, occasionally taking them out and reading them over and over. The first one is from Lynn, her best friend. It was written at graveside during one of her visits and then given to me.

March 2, 1999

Dearest Marcy,

As I sit here next to your grave my eyes water and my nose begins to run as I think about everything, the good times we had and the memories made. I look at your picture on the stone. You look so alive. How could this be? Five years…

I remember…your turquoise bedroom, all your pictures in nice neat albums (your mom trained you well). You then trained me on how to put pictures in albums and label every single one. You would be happy to know that I still carry on this tradition with my children's pictures.

I remember…youth groups, high school, sleepovers, Friday night dinners at my parents' house, late nights at your house and New Year's Eve with Near Beer (that famous non-alcoholic beer that makes kids feel like they're older). Thanks to your grandma who supplied it. We thought we were so cool. We even gave a friend the beer and told her it was real. We laughed when she started pretending she was tipsy. Oh, did she look silly!

I remember…the summer in Israel, boyfriends here and there, all the letters from home, the kleptomaniac in our group. I remember your A.S.U. dorm, your condo and parties you had. I remember all the traveling, plays, new experiences. Sometimes we traveled together, sometimes with other friends. But we always kept in touch.

I remember…for our 19th birthday we went to London for a month with your dad's mom, Grandma Ora. When we needed space from her on a trip to Windemere, England, we rented a row boat with a motor, packed our lunch and enjoyed being on the beautiful lake, just the two of us together. We laughed, basked in the sun and relaxed. I think it was one of our special private times together.

Remember how fascinated we were with all the kinds of beer in England, the colorful cans they came in and the interesting names. So we bought, drank and collected them. We chose our beers not based on how good the ale was supposed to be, but by the colorful container it came in and the uniqueness of the name. After sipping we dumped the rest, kept the containers and lugged all the empty cans home to display at our apartments. Do you know I still have mine? They line the top shelf of my old room at my parent's home.

Los Angeles…what great times we had there together and after I moved back to Phoenix, I still took monthly trips there to see you. I remember your first roommate was weird; friends and boyfriends moved to L.A.; you learned your parents were splitting up; birthday parties rocked at the beach; and then your grandmother died. We went through it all together from the time we first met at the Temple youth group during our trip to Disneyland. We shared a pillow on the bus. That was the start of our very special friendship.

My regret is that we were never roommates. I think I would have really liked that. We wanted our kids to grow up together and the four of us to travel the world. We had great plans, didn't we, to spend lots of time growing old together. It was not to be.

We never thought about death…it never really occurred to us. I know your folks miss you terribly as I and many others do. We don't keep in touch with Simon, unfortunately, but I'm sure he misses you as well.

You'd be happy to know, Marcy, that your parents play a huge role in my children's lives. You cared, loved and cherished your parents so much, but you don't have to worry. They are an important part of my life now too. Please pass the pictures I leave with you of the children on to them when they come to visit today.

I guess I'm on a trip down memory lane, but this is what this day is all about for me…remembering. Since I have been cheated out of the last five years and all the years to come, I remember all the years we had together.

I can't believe it's been so long since I saw your smile, heard your laugh, hugged and talked to you. I miss you, Marcy, and always will.

Lots and lots of love,
Lynn

P.S. I still have all the cards you gave me.

"I wrote this letter at the cemetery on March 2 and left it and part of my heart there with Marcy. She died a week after my wedding, the day Marc and I were leaving on our honeymoon.

We switched planes in Los Angeles, so I called to thank her for her message the night before wishing us a good trip. Her office told me what had happened. I began shaking so badly and crying, Marc knew something horrible had happened. I think I was in complete shock. The honeymoon was cancelled.

"As I speak with my mom or dad who are now in their sixties or with others and see relationships they have with their best friends from years past, I can't help but find myself envious, a little jealous and longing for that relationship and feeling I had with my best friend. It was one I cherished and dearly miss.

"When I look back at all the letters and cards I saved from Marcy, one common thread runs through them all. She always ended her notes by writing "Your best bud, Marcy." One in particular, the last one I got from her on my 27th birthday said, "We both got engaged this year. Oh, my God, we're not old maids together! Can you believe you'll be Mrs. Lerner this time next year. What a lucky babe UR! Your best bud, Marcy." (Marcy was married four months before me.) I miss my birthday cards from Marcy. I pull old ones out each year and read them. It helps.

"Since the moment Marcy died, my heart feels like it has a huge hole in it and a coldness passes through me every time I think of her. At first I cried a lot, I slept a lot and then I cried some more. I didn't know how Marc could stand being with me. I thought about why we're on this earth, why some people go on living, others die. Then a selfish thought: Why Marcy? It's not fair. For a while I really wished it had been me. I kept saying this over and over. I know it was hard for Marc to hear this. But it was how I felt. At that time in her life Marcy was really going places. She was bright, quick, friendly and kind. I didn't want to die, but I sure as hell didn't want Marcy to die either.

"I went in and out of denial. I thought of her every day and sometimes even believed that she was beside me. I had visions right after she died that she was talking to me and leading me on. It was comforting but empty because I couldn't hug her.

"I lost weight. I visited a psychiatrist. I couldn't get rid of this painful hole in me and wanted to know if it was always going to be like this. Marc was and is so patient and kind, so loving, helpful and understanding. I was a mess, but he helped me through it.

"I finally decided that Marcy would be so pissed at me if I messed up my relationship with Marc. She liked him so much. When we told her of our engagement she had Marc on the phone alone and laid down the rules of taking care of me, loving me and all the info about me he needed to know. If anyone could set a person straight, it was Marcy.

"As the years pass, the tears and pain lessen. The hole in my heart will never completely mend, and that is okay. I learn to live with it. From life's experiences I've come to terms with her death. I used to believe that everything had a reason for happening. Now I question that rationale. I understand how life can be cut short so quickly, and

I know that to move on with my life I must accept death, at any age, as a fact of life.

"I love you Marcy. You will always have a very special place in the corner of my heart."

* * *

Andrea, one of Marcy's roommates in Los Angeles, expressed her deep feelings in the following letter sent to me.

"Gregarious, generous, good listener, concerned about friend's well-being, high-energy, vibrant, creative, positive, supportive and honest. Those are the adjectives I think of when I want to describe Marcy. It's very rare to get that in many friends. I was one of the fortunate ones.

"Marcy and I knew each other 5 1/2 years. We were roommates in Los Angeles; we socialized together; we talked for hours about every subject possible. She became my best friend. Although I know she had several best friends, that never took away any love or energy she had for our friendship; she had enough for everyone. Her death left a void in me that may never be filled.

"I heard about Marcy's death at work. My roommate, Lori, called. She was screaming and crying on the phone. I couldn't believe it either. I had just talked to her the night before. How could this be, I kept asking myself.

"I remember the night she died I was home alone feeling melancholy. I went running, came back, sat around for some time and then looked at the clock. It was 7 p.m. (the time Marcy died.) I could sense something strange. I believe when you are very close to someone, you do that. At 9 p.m. I called her because I was upset about a relationship problem and left a message. I didn't sleep well that night. And then the news. Did I somehow deep down know?

"The first day all her friends and many relatives pulled together at my apartment. That was comforting since I never got to say goodbye. By the second day, three of us went to the accident site with a candle and flowers. I needed to face it; it was hard. I stood there and tried to imagine what happened, and did the "what if's." What if Simon had picked her up a few minutes later. What if she had driven to work that day. What if the tree had not been there. But you can "what if" yourself to death, and it doesn't change what happened.

"For all our friends, her death was so devastating. I believe there are two reasons for this. First, we were all at a stage in our lives that everything was starting to click for us. Then you think, "This could be me." Second, in today's society we have so much technology that we live under the illusion we have control of our lives, and we don't. It is a real eye opener and very frightening.

"I feel privileged and honored to have known Marcy and to have experienced her vibrant personality. After knowing her, I can truly say I know what a best friend is, one who can give you unconditional love and understanding. Marcy was so supportive of me and what I did. She was always there to listen, give advice and be honest the way a friend should be. She was instrumental in getting my future husband and I together. But she was up front about the situation. "You're going to be just friends first," Marcy told me, "so don't expect too much too soon; he does like you a lot; he's just very shy." Marcy was right, and it was six months before he asked me out. I appreciated her telling it like it was, then and always.

"Since Marcy's death I have experienced other close deaths including my father and grandmother, but none has touched me the way Marcy's did. I think of her often to give me strength to get through whatever bad situation I am in at the time. Marcy had an incredible gift for always looking at the bright side and picking me up when I was down. Because of this gift our friendship will be everlasting and Marcy will always be in my heart and thoughts.

"What helped the first year was all our friends getting together. I had my own friends, but her friends were mine too. She was good at sharing her friends. I did a collage of pictures of my friends and put her in it.

Why shouldn't I? Just because she is no longer with us, she is and will always be my friend.

"On the first anniversary of her death a group of our friends recognized the day and went ice-skating. It was a celebration of sorts. We were celebrating her life, and we liked to talk about her. It was good for all of us, but especially me. As the years go on, the pain lessens, but the good memories will always be there. And I still love to talk about her.

"I think Marcy's concern for her friends is what I will always remember most. In 1992 three of us took a trip to Boston. I was on a very strict budget and Marcy knew it. She was so careful to make sure we didn't go over $33 a person per day, even though she and the other girl could afford more. She even found a YWCA for us, much to the dismay of our companion. When I got a job that paid more the following year Marcy was so happy for me. She was always supportive for making my life better.

"Marcy's untimely and unfair death will always be a lump in my throat; however, her memory, her laugh and smile will always be a bright light in my life as I remember her. She brought many people together and touched me in a way that can never be forgotten. I often think of the following quote by May Sarton when I remember Marcy: "*She became for me an island of light, fun, and wisdom where I could run with my discoveries, torments and hopes at any time of day and find welcome.*"

* * *

Larry, her boss at work, gave a beautiful eulogy at her funeral. His thoughts afterwards showed her creativity and kindness.

"I will never work with anyone who was more of a friend to others. Marcy was a catalyst. She was special.

"I remember the first day we met when I interviewed her for a job at the Music Center in Los Angeles in 1988. I had received many resumes for an assistant marketing director, Marcy being one of them. We talked on the phone and followed up with a personal visit. I remember that Marcy told me she had driven to the Music Center the previous day to find where to park. She scouted out the freeways, the parking lot and the building she needed to go to. That was a good sign of her common sense. I remember a candidate who was late. I called her house to find out when she didn't show up, got an answering machine and left the message, "What happened?" Later this person called to say, "I didn't know where to park." Marcy was 45 minutes early for her interview. She got the job.

"With all of the events, clubs, projects, publications and festivals, everyone in my department needed to work together. We adopted a system for hiring. I would find the two best candidates and let the group choose their favorite. We, including Marcy, voted almost every time together. She was excellent at evaluating people. I miss her insights.

"During 1989, the 25th Anniversary of the Music Center, we invited Charlton Heston to come say "Happy Birthday" and a few words about performing at the theaters on our plaza. When brainstorming in our marketing department we came up with a creative idea to have Charlton part the plaza fountain waters, as Moses did in the movie **The Ten Commandments.** Charlton came, brought a wooden scepter, said some words and the waters parted. It all worked. The crowd loved it, and so did the press. When he wanted to leave, Marcy and I walked him to his car. When we got to his limousine it was locked and the driver not to be found. We all panicked when Charlton started getting mobbed for his autograph. After what seemed like 30 minutes of looking and keeping Charlton from blowing up, we found the driver and off they went. I remember Marcy got a few words from the driver. He said that he was so interested in what we were doing on the plaza that he left the limousine to watch not only the parting of the waters but the music, other stars and food given out to everyone.

"Marcy and I were brainstorming one day because the famous musician YoYo Ma was coming. Our objective was to build the audiences on the plaza in downtown L.A. So we looked at each other and said, "Let's call Duncan yo-yo's! They would be fun for giveaways and demonstrations. We called the Philharmonic and they said, "Are you nuts?" Marcy and I talked a few times about that story and "our" creativity.

"I heard about Marcy's death from a phone call at home. I remember driving to work in a fog, not believing that the night before we were laughing and chatting, waiting for Simon to pick her up. They were going out to celebrate the purchase of a new car.

"One of the special moments in my life was when I spoke about Marcy at the cemetery. I treasure the time we had together.

"I talked with a hundred people at the Music Center so that we could have a stone with Marcy's name near the fountain. With others in the office we debated for hours about where the stone should go. Should it be nearest the fountain, the dance door sculpture or the shop, one of Marcy's own marketing projects? It was decided to put it near the flow of traffic and nearest our office and the Mark Taper Forum. It was a special moment all of us thinking and feeling about Marcy and deciding on that special stone for Marcy to be remembered by all of us and visitors to the Music Center."

* * *

I sensed Kathy and Anne, close co-workers, felt more than just a deep loss. Kathy expressed it this way.

"Marcy was one of the "sparkliest," loveliest people to ever become a significant part of my life…but it is very painful for me, since her death remains one of the most untimely tragedies I have ever witnessed.

"I can't picture Marcy without a smile; she was always amused by something, teasing me about something or just enjoying life in general. She was so incredibly happy with Simon, and I am so grateful that she was able to experience that relationship, with all of its joy, before she was taken away from us. I used to tease her and Simon that they were so "sickeningly sweet" together that they gave me an upset stomach! The last time I saw her was shortly after my younger son, Josh, was born, and she and Simon came to visit us. They brought him a beautiful little outfit, and I was never able to put that clothing on him without crying. Needless to say, I have saved the outfit and will cherish it always.

"That day, while we were visiting, she and Simon were sort of verbally experimenting with the concept of becoming parents, what it would be like, how they would handle parenting. I have often thought what an exceptionally joyous mother Marcy would have become, and how sad it is that it will never be.

"Marcy was not only one of the most intelligent people I have ever had the joy to know and love, but she was also one of the most thoughtful. My older son, Jason, adored her, and she was so careful to talk with him and play with him.

"I'll never forget something that happened right before her wedding. She called me in a total panic because she was "breaking out" from the stress of preparing for the wedding. I told her to go get a facial and then use a blemish control gel I had. She came and got it from me, and the combination worked. Her complexion was glowing the day of the wedding! The day after the wedding, my husband and I left our house early but when we came home, she had delivered the blemish control gel back to me as they were on their way to their honeymoon! She wanted to make certain I had the gel in case I needed it while they were gone. How many new brides would be that thoughtful?

"Marcy came to feel like a little sister to me and burrowed her way deeper into my heart than just about any friendship I have formed in my adult years. Even after I stopped working at the Music Center, we talked almost daily, usually about something totally unimportant, but always to just stay connected. While she was planning her wedding, she would call me with "etiquette" questions. She used to tease me and call me "Miss Manners," and it was so adorable how she wanted everything at her wedding and reception to be just perfect, in a very traditional sort of way. She was even late to her reception because she stopped in the dining room to make sure all the table set-ups were correct and discovering they weren't, stayed to fix them.

"I am still to this day greatly troubled by her death, and it has been a regular subject in my ongoing debates with God. It has become part of my grappling with issues of faith and eternity and the reasons we are here and what God intends...all of those complex concepts that I'm sure I'll be debating until God takes me as well.

"Some random memories of Marcy: she had a remarkable memory, never forgot anything; she was a terrific assistant, because she never hesitated to ask questions, always the right ones, or question something that didn't make sense to her, didn't look right, sound right, feel right. She was never a *yes* man, and it was wonderful to have that kind of support, have another intelligent mind double-checking everything that went through the marketing department at the Music Center.

"Losing Marcy was remarkably painful for me. The day Larry, her boss, got the call, he decided he wouldn't be able to get the words out. They called my husband who, in turn, called me. I remember that my nanny came into the room, holding Josh (a newborn at the time), and when I hung up the phone, I asked to hold him. I sat there sobbing and rocked him for a very long, long time. I couldn't picture the world without her, and, to this day, something deep down inside me still doesn't believe it.

"Marcy was a shining, shimmering, delightful light of a human being, and I miss her every day."

Anne's letter said, "At the time I worked with Marcy, she was unique among my friends for her sheer joy for life. She fully enjoyed life and wholeheartedly embraced it, the downs as well as the ups, more than anyone I knew.

"She brought a zest to her work, finding something amusing even in the most mundane of tasks, and a warmth and steady affection to her relationships with her friends. I used to marvel at what I considered her energy and exuberance, attributing it to her youth. But now, looking back, I know it was much more than simple energy. Marcy truly enjoyed each and every day. She expected the best out of life, and was more often than not rewarded for that trust.

"I have been lucky enough thus far to have had little experience with death, but Marcy's seemed a particular travesty. Her life was so filled with promise, and she had so much love and joy to give that her senseless death seemed especially appalling. What a waste for someone who so loved life to be taken away in such an incredibly stupid manner!

"What has Marcy left me? So much more than just fond memories. Marcy's death came a month before the birth of my first child, a daughter. Of course, her untimely death left me with a determination to "live everyday to the fullest," as the old cliche goes. But, more significantly, her death left me with a real determination to instill that same sense of love for life in my daughter and subsequent children.

"Marcy lived her life in a way I, and most people, never really do, with the greatest joy and exuberance. You see this same quality in babies and small children, who greet each day with a big smile, sure that it will bring nothing but joy. You almost never see this in adults, though. My goal in raising my children is to maintain and strengthen this quality, this natural exuberance for life.

"That has meant I've had to change how I live my life. Children follow and learn by example and it is by this example that I want to guide their lives. That has meant slowing down, enjoying each experience for what it's worth, remembering that this truly is the happiest time of my life, and making sure that I convey this joy and love to those around me, especially my children.

"I truly believe that this is Marcy's gift to me: a knowledge that life can be as full and joyful as I want to make it, and a real determination to instill this same belief in my children. For that, I will be eternally grateful to Marcy, and through my life, I hope to honor hers."

*　　　*　　　*

Marcy was not only friendly with one sister, but two. Susan, Lynn's older sister, to this day has a lot of trouble dealing with Marcy's death. In her words:

"Marcy had an energy about her. She was very personable. I feel towards Marcy as I would for a little sister. When I think of her, I remember the young teenager cohorting and planning with my younger sister, Lynn. For as long as I remember, the two were best friends.

"I'll never forget some of the last times Marcy and I shared together. Lynn's wedding was coming up, and we were both bridesmaids.We went to a dressmaker together to see about having our dresses made. I didn't know what my waist line would be by the time of the wedding; I was one month pregnant. She was one of the first to know.

"We planned a party for the engaged couple. Marcy had ordered the invitations. Later on when I wanted to get more of the stationery we had used, I realized that I couldn't just call her and ask where she had gotten it. It was too late.

"One evening Marcy and Simon had a party at their condo. His name was finally included in the credits as executive producer for "Look Who's Talking" after a long court battle. They had a small condo on a second floor that had outdoor hallways. The party spilled over from the living room into the hallway. We watched the section of the movie that showed the credits, and when Simon's name appeared, everyone cheered. I remember thinking what a special group of people this was, how easily Marcy made friends and how many friends she had made in the short time of living in a new city.

"The last time I saw Marcy was at Lynn's wedding. I'll never forget her attentiveness to Lynn that day. What a good friend she was! We had all arrived at the bridal lounge early to get ready and have pictures taken before the ceremony. She brought all of us orange juice and bagels. Throughout the morning she kept feeding Lynn to make sure she had enough energy for the upcoming activities. These are my last memories of her: being a supportive, dedicated, loving friend.

"The phone call is indelibly etched in my mind. I was told at my office that Marcy had been in a car accident. I asked how she was, thinking maybe she had a broken bone. The response was "She's dead." I must have screamed because the next thing I knew a friend came in from the next office. He held me while I cried uncontrollably. For a long time afterward whenever I saw a car accident, I would start crying or get choked up. I felt numb, detached and my heart ached.

"Marcy's death was the most painful experience in my life. Even today, almost seven years later, I've cried throughout writing this. Whenever I think of her, my eyes tear up and my heart aches. It just doesn't seem right. Marcy was so young. She never reached her 30th birthday. For her, the timing of a mid-life crisis would be the same time as puberty.

"I have experienced a lot of deaths. Usually, the intensity of the feeling of loss subsides eventually, and I feel that the person lives on in our memories and through how they have shaped our lives. I have not yet reached this point with Marcy's death. I don't know if you ever fully recover from a loss like this. Just some of the symptoms subside so that we can go on with our lives."

*　　　*　　　*

For many weeks after the accident I reveled in the words and thoughts from her friends and co-workers. I decided to put many of these thoughts into booklet form and give to those who would enjoy having the remembrances and slowly began the task which would take about four months.This booklet was separate from some of the more recent letters I have included here.

While I was doing this, a great fear surfaced. Everyone was sympathetic to my loss, memorials were held, but I knew eventually they would go back to their lives and the mourning would cease. Would everyone forget she ever existed? I did not want that to happen, and apparently neither did others, I discovered. What started as a great tribute to her at the Los Angeles Music Center turned into many memorials around the western part of the country and perhaps in years to come, others like Marcy will benefit from what Marcy did not live long enough to enjoy herself.

At my school the SADD group (Students Against Distructive Decisions) bought a beautiful Jacaronda tree and planted it alongside my classroom, a symbol of life everlasting. With it, teachers and SADD placed a plaque in her memory under the tree with her name and date on it. Even though I retired, I still visit it when I can.

Marcy's boss, Larry, who loved Marcy like a daughter and thought she was the most creative, most organized employee he ever had, helped to organize and hold a memorial evening for every worker at the center.The Music Center president at the time said, "I knew we had to do something. It seemed like no one could function again until they had some closure." Both Jess and I were invited and flew to L.A. for the event. Larry also made sure that a plaque in memory of Marcy was placed in the water fountain courtyard of the Dorothy Chandler Pavilion in downtown Los Angeles. I thought this a great feat, since, to get your name on a marble stone there you had to either be famous or a special contributor to the arts. Marcy's co-workers and friends in Los Angeles must have thought she was very special, because they contributed enough money to see that it happened, and Larry made it all come true. She would be pleased where her memorial stone is, right before the water actually falls, in clear view of anyone looking for it. It will be there forever.

Since she was a lover of the arts and had spent so much of her high school years in and around theater, Michael and I dedicated a stone in her memory at the remodeled Orpheum Theater in downtown Phoenix. Her stone sits next to all the ones from former and present mayors of the city. She is in good company.

Marcy loved Maui. Michael and I bought six stones at the Maui Arts and Cultural Center there that read "Michael J. Fox, Sandy R. Fox, In

Memory of Beloved Daughter, Marcy Jeanne Finerman Lewis." Every time we visit the island it is one important stop.

When the Arizona Diamondback franchise became a reality in Phoenix, memorial stones were sold at the entrance to the stadium. We bought one in memory of Marcy and also one with Michael's and my name on it.

But it is in Camp Charles Pearlstein in the Prescott, Arizona, mountains where hundreds of children spend their summers that her best friend, Lynn, raised enough money to have a drama and recreation center built and named after her, the Marcy Jeanne Finerman Lewis Memorial Drama Center. Many family members and friends were there for the dedication as the camp children sang songs and performed on the stage next to where the plaque naming the center is placed in her honor.

Jess has started an endowment fund to eventually provide scholarships to students who want to pursue careers in the entertainment field. At the high school I taught in for 28 years, a journalism scholarship was set up in her name for many years, helping students in college eager to get into the newspaper or broadcast business.

We who loved her so will not let anyone forget. We are proud to hear from students who have used the scholarships and theater well. Marcy had many dreams she was never able to fulfill. I hope that with these many memorials, Marcy's heart will be content. I know my heart is at peace from all these wonderful people and things that were done. More than anything it has helped me to heal within and move forward.

8

Afterwards

"They shall not grow old as we that are left.
Age shall not weary them, nor the years condemn that the going down of the sun.
And in the morning we will remember them."

from Reform Judaism Prayerbook

On January 15, 1999, the same day my daughter got engaged to Simon six years earlier, Lynn gave birth to a second child, a girl. She and husband Marc named her Marcy. The circle of life continues...

PART 2

Other Parents' Stories

1

Matthew

"There is new growth out of this devastation. I am doing things now that I never thought I was capable of doing...I started sharing my son's story on college campuses...so others wouldn't have to suffer what my family suffered and continues to endure..."

Maxine

I am standing in front of the auditorium in the high school from which my three sons graduated. Filling the seats in front of me are the members of the junior and senior classes. The date is March 9, 1999, the sixth anniversary of my middle son Matthew's funeral. I am about to do something I never thought I would be capable of doing. I am about to share my deepest sorrow with these young people. I am about to relate to them how Matthew died with the hope that these young people will learn from his fatal mistake.

I believe children have power over their parents, the power to cause the greatest joy and the deepest pain. But, I never truly felt the reality of that statement until Matthew died on March 7, 1993. Over the years, I had derived a lot of joy from my three sons, and I had always anticipated the happiness I would glean from them in the future, as they continued to grow, to accomplish and to reach so many milestones in their journey to manhood and beyond. That is not to say that I hadn't felt the emotions at the opposite end of the spectrum as well. I had felt pain and fear as a result of various serious illnesses that they suffered and disappointment as a result of certain deeds that they had done. My children are not perfect.

In the years before Matthew died, whenever I heard about a child that had died, my heart ached for his or her parents. I could never imagine how any individual could go on living after such a tragedy. I just knew, from deep within my being, that nothing could be worse than this. Yet, until I had to endure it myself, I never realized the depth of this pain. When Matthew first died, I just didn't know how I would be able to go on living. But I did. And I've continued to live. It is not the same living as before his death, but I am alive, and I do function in what I describe as an altered state.

Matthew's life was taking him in the right direction. He graduated with honors from high school, doing well athletically as well as scholastically. He had gotten into the University of Florida's Honors Program. He majored in Spanish and was toying with the possibility of living and working in Spain after he graduated. He had so much potential, so many plans and so many dreams. They were wiped out by his lack of judgment and lack of understanding of the consequences of his actions. He died of alcohol poisoning, never even knowing that someone could die in this way.

Matthew's death devastated all of us, his immediate family, consisting of my husband of 28 years, Joe, and me and his brothers Rob, 19 months his senior, and Jon, 5 1/2 years his junior, and those in his extended family of relatives and friends. Part of me died with him. I will never be the same person I was before. How could I be? I buried a child that I had borne. I had to see him carried out of my home in a body bag. I had to arrange for his funeral. And, in the Jewish tradition, I shoveled dirt onto his coffin after it was lowered into his grave.

I don't recall in detail how I got through those initial years of grief. I do know that it was the hardest thing I have ever had to do. Many people comment that at least we all had each other. But we didn't. Each of us was grieving separately, not as a family unit. This is to be expected, since each of us is different and each of us had our own unique relationship with Matt. I was paralyzed by my own grief, oblivious to my family's needs. I couldn't help Rob and Jonathan, my other two sons, and I had difficulty sharing my feelings with Joe.

I don't even recall preparing meals. My husband had opened a take-out restaurant just before Matt died, and I was preparing cakes for him to sell. I recall coming home from work everyday and baking. It was almost therapeutic. I only had to think about measuring ingredients, mixing them together, putting the cakes in the oven and decorating them when they were done. I didn't have to think about my son who had died.

I found The Compassionate Friends and another parental bereavement support group run by a local hospital to be of immense help to me. I looked forward to those two monthly meetings. They got me through the month. It was there I could reveal my deepest feelings and get the understanding that only another bereaved parent could offer.

I learned to do only that which I was comfortable doing. I went back to work after the mourning period. I found that to be quite helpful. Being out of the house was good. Even though Matthew was on my mind most of the time, I was able to carry out my responsibilities. And when I was overcome by the enormity of what had happened, I would close my office door, and I would cry.

I did not go to social functions. I couldn't. My husband and I tried twice, and had to leave early both times. Thus, a decision was made not to go until we were both ready, not when others thought we should be ready, but when we knew it was possible to go without too much discomfort. We continued on as best we could, but it was so hard.

Now there is new growth out of this devastation. I am doing things now that I never thought I was capable of doing. Approximately a year and a half after Matthew's death, I started sharing his story on college campuses. I didn't want any other family to have to suffer what my family suffered and continues to endure. I wanted young people to understand how the effects of their irresponsible choices impact on all who love them. My message comes across to them. I've had young people share their own stories of alcohol related loss and some have told me about their own close brushes with alcohol poisoning. At the time of the incidents, they never realized the risk they were putting themselves in. They also never realized how their actions affect all who love them.

I usually ask for comments and questions after I finish speaking. Many times there is just silence when I am done. However, I have had students and faculty share some very moving stories with me. One incident that was particularly powerful occurred about a year and a half ago. After I finished my talk, with one of two extremely emotional poems written by my son Jonathan, a young woman in tears got up to speak. The woman, a senior, told of the time, as a freshman, she had been binge drinking. She passed out and her friends video taped her. She was lucky enough to wake up the next morning and when her friends showed her the tape, she was appalled. She remembered nothing of what she saw. Her friends were posing her and she hadn't a clue. She said she looked near death. Yet, as upset as she was with seeing herself in that state, it wasn't until she heard me talk approximately three years later, that she realized what could have happened to her and how it would have devastated her family and friends. If I reach just one person each time I speak, I've accomplished something. She was my one person at that session.

Another time, a high school teacher told me of the time her son was hospitalized with alcohol poisoning. He was lucky. He lived. And there are so many other stories as well. As much as my audiences are grateful to me for sharing, I am grateful to them. Through my talking, I can share Matthew with them, and so he is accomplishing something, while not in life, at least in death.

More recently, I have become involved in a local Community Task Force which was formed in response to the underage drinking taking place in our town. I've taken part in the formulation and presentation of programs to students and parents dealing with various alcohol related issues, in particular alcohol poisoning. And all along I have continued to be a part of The Compassionate Friends. At first I relied on the monthly meetings to help me get through the worst of the grief process. Then, as I was able to, I took on a more active role in the leadership of the group, becoming a chapter co-leader and editor of its newsletter.

Before Matthew's death I would never have imagined myself doing any of these activities, but the new me needs to. So whether it's speaking to a group of people, with Matt's photo staring up at me from beside my notes to give me strength, or if it's sitting at the computer in Matt's room and working on the Compassionate Friends newsletter or preparing for a meeting, I believe that I am getting my strength from my son Matthew. And while I am proud of what I am doing and what I continue to be part of, the bottom line is "Would I go back to the old me if I could have Matt back?" In a millisecond.

Observations of Maxine

Maxine gives us a good picture of the overwhelming grief that consumes a person when a child dies and how that parent can turn his or her grief around to make something good come out of such a tragedy. This doesn't happen immediately. Grief can be so disabling, it can take years to get the courage to even face the possibility that you will survive. You have lost part of yourself; you have lost your future. When your child is torn from you, you change. You find a way to live your life without your child as Maxine did, yet you want to feel the child in everything you do. So you reassemble a world in which you can live.

To Maxine, finding pleasure and rebuilding her life took the form of helping others through two venues, The Compassionate Friends and speaking on campuses in hopes of alleviating other unnecessary deaths. In The Compassionate Friends she has found understanding, friendship and support from other bereaved parents. There she learned that feeling such acute pain, helplessness and "what ifs" are not unusual for most families. They are more the norm. In her talks to students and parents she tries to get the message across about how precious life is and when you do something irresponsible you hurt everyone around you by your actions.

As she prepares these presentations and sees the faces of her audience anticipating what she will say, she is comforted in knowing her passionate cause has found an outlet in those willing to listen and hopefully, to take action.

2

Michael

> *"As a member of Parents of Murdered Children, I speak to victim volunteers in local police departments. I teach them how to deal with survivors, the do's and don't's for communicating..."*
>
> Veronica

It was a botched burglary by three men. My son and grandson shot.

"Tell me it's not true. Tell me my boys are okay," I screamed at the policeman.

"I'm sorry, madam, they're dead."

My knees gave out. A policeman caught me. My husband went ballistic and tried to punch out the window of the police car. I replay that moment often, one of the few I remember in that horror-filled time of my life, 1994.

My 27-year-old son, Michael, and his son, 8-year-old Joshua, were innocently gunned down by men high on drugs probably needing money for more drugs. My son struggled with them but was shot multiple times. My grandson was shot once in the head.

Michael was a single parent at the time living in a triplex owned by his father. Because of the long hours he worked in the food industry,

Joshua lived with my husband and I during the week and his dad on weekends. That week the regular routine was broken when I didn't insist Josh come to my house. Michael had been out of town and wanted to see him that night. How ironic that he and his son died at the hands of drug users. Michael had always been concerned about the drug problem and his son growing up in this era of abuse.

One gunman died in a police chase car accident within a month of the robbery. Through the drug community and talk on the streets, the other two were caught 11 months later. After years of legal maneuvering one was eventually set free. The other was convicted of only Joshua's murder. I presented an impact statement prior to the sentencing. In the statement I addressed a number of issues and discussed my personal loss.

"*I'll never again see their smiling faces, feel the big man bear hugs or the little boy's soft embrace. I'll never hear them say, 'I love you.'*" I talked about seeing their lifeless bodies in their caskets, looking so unlike themselves in life. And the future-devoid of joy. "*I no longer look forward, I just am.*" I talked of the loss to other members of the family as well as Michael's and Josh's friends. I told who Michael and Josh were…loving, caring human beings and Michael's willingness to help others. I discussed the defendant's family dysfunction that permeated the judicial process and called it a cop out. "*I do not personally know anyone who grew up in a perfect family. I certainly did not. Yet not one of the individuals I personally know who grew up in a dysfunctional family committed crimes against other persons as a result.*" And finally, to the defendant, I said that by his actions he destroyed not only my family but also his own. "*As a result, I will never forget you and what you took from me. But I will not allow your existence to consume me. By your actions the killer of an 8-year-old boy walks the streets a free man.*" I spoke of God and how I turned my bitterness and hate over to Him and asked Him to give me peace and comfort along this difficult journey, leaving my fate in His hands. I ended my address to him with "*May God have mercy on your soul.*"

He ended up serving only 24 days in prison. He died of a cerebral hemorrhage. No one was ever held responsible for Michael's death.

Our reactions when the police told us what had happened that night they were murdered was quite opposite of our personalities. I am usually the vocal one but at that point was completely numb and in a state of shock. My husband, who is a quiet person, was the one who went out of control.

Michael was a very private person, had a great sense of humor and was very laid back. He had one other child, a son, who lived with his mother. The "white knight" he was called, when he tried to help others, particularly intervening in domestic fights. He helped women by providing a place for them to stay. I later found out he even helped one of my co-workers.

Michael and my husband, his stepfather, were just starting to get along well. There was the natural resentment at first since I was married to Michael's father for 16 years. But it was my husband and grandchild who were very close and did a lot together. Step-parents are often misunderstood, but my husband loved them both very much. He wrote once, "Love comes from the heart, not from the blood it pumps."

I don't remember much of that first year after his death. I didn't feel part of the human race. It was like I was on the outside looking in on it. My heart physically hurt. I felt like I had a hole in my soul. For the first six months I would open my eyes in the morning, so disappointed I was still alive. The pain was so deep I did not want to live, even though my daughter, two years younger, needed me. Most nights I could not sleep. I kept replaying everything that had happened, the pain, the agony, the vision of what they must have looked like afterwards. It is only this last year that I have slept all night through.

I had many guilt feelings. I had told Michael the area they lived in was a bad one. "Get out," I kept telling him. They were in the process of finding a new place to move. But it wasn't in time. I didn't insist Josh come to my house that night, and I should have. Anger was there, but there was not much room for it because I was so filled with grief and guilt.

In that first year I read some books on the grieving process. ***No Time for Goodbyes*** was good, but I could not get into it, nor did I feel uplifted when I read ***When Bad Things Happen To Good People.*** After I reached the acceptance stage of the grieving process, and knew they would never be coming back, I turned to "life after death" books. I wanted to know when I would see them again.

I am still not totally comfortable in a crowd. I don't have any friends that are not in the organization, Parents of Murdered Children, the group that was able to finally help me. Most people treat me like I have a disease, and I am contagious. I do realize it's hard for people to understand my grief and know what to say, but to avoid me completely was just too much. So my husband and I stick to socializing with friends we've made from the organization.

It was a long, hard process to get where I am today. Statistics show that it takes 7-9 years for parents to recover from a homicide. Not a day goes by that I don't think about them. You learn to live with the pain, learn to function, learn what to say to who so they won't see inside you. You put on a mask for the world and take it off for those who understand.

My relationship with my husband changed initially because everyone grieves alone. You have to learn to respect the other's right to grieve in their own time. My husband and I go to the cemetery together and cry together. When we come home we go off by ourselves. It works for us.

Two months after the murders, personnel came into my office at Macy's where I worked at the time and gave me the phone number of Parents of Murdered Children. I went to the meetings where they explained to me my reaction was normal. I wasn't going insane. When I would be driving and realized I didn't know where I was going, I panicked. That, too, was normal, they said. I found a comfort level with the group; they have been there, done that. People at work know what happened, but we don't talk about it.

Within this group I have become very active. I now speak to victim volunteers in various local police departments. This program is for those who died violently or in an accident. I teach volunteers how to deal with survivors, the do's and don't's for communicating with them. I also speak to other groups in the city. On weekends I am a 'phone friend.' I call in to the message center three times a day to pick up messages from parents who want information, who need help or who need a speaker. I am the east side grief support facilitator, and I call members at home if they are having a particular problem.

There are two meetings a month for Parents of Murdered Children. At the first meeting there is usually a speaker such as a medical examiner or a police officer. The second meeting is a support group meeting where parents can vent their feelings and know others understand.

Working with this group makes me feel good, knowing that I can give back what was given to me. It helps me to help others. These are great people who had horrendous things happen to them.

It was a long, hard process to get where I am today. I would advise anyone who has gone through this to reach out to groups where people have had the same experience. They can understand where you're at. They don't take the pain away, but they can walk along beside you and steady you a little as you walk down the path.

Observations of Veronica

Because of Veronica's plight with the criminal justice system being more than frustrating, her grieving period dragged on for a long time. It took four years for at least one of the men accused of her son's and grandson's murder to be put on trial, convicted and sentenced. Veronica couldn't believe it when he was found innocent of her son's murder, yet guilty of her grandson's. She wanted justice and to see this person punished for what was done to both her loved ones. But it was not to be. When he died in prison, it was a blessing, according to Veronica. He had filed an appeal and chances looked good he would have gotten a new trial. She was glad not to have to go through it again. Trials can be emotionally draining and frustrating to a victim's family, as it was to Veronica's.

Families have a choice. They may work within the criminal justice system and be an active player, or they may prefer not to become involved. Participating can help with gaining control over one's life, though it will not make what happened or the judicial system any easier to bear. Not participating can keep your emotional level on an even keel and your journey to recovery easier, or it may result in buried emotions surfacing later.

New laws have been put into effect in the last few years. Written Victim Impact Statements can be submitted to the prosecutor or probation department before a hearing to consider a plea bargain or sentencing. Some states allow oral statements. These statements testify about the emotional impact the crime had on your life, as well as the financial impact including medical expenses, funeral expenses, lost wages and any counseling expenses resulting from the trauma.

Other states notify victim's families about possible parole hearings and allow testimony. Still others allow opinions as to what kind of sentence should be given, although that is not the case in Arizona. Laws differ from state to state, so checking what is and what is not allowed is essential.

Veronica, like others, will never forget what happened, but in the company of those who have gone through the same ordeal she finds comfort and understanding.

3

Dave

"We found that the friends who were helpful were the ones who weren't afraid of us...These people led us into what we needed to do, talk and cry about it. Others were anxious for our grieving to be over. These people don't have a clue how this all works..."

Karl

When my wife Sue and I travel, if it is a special place, we leave some of Dave's ashes. I pick up a stone as a remembrance of a beautiful place I think Dave would have liked and place it in my pocket. Dave, my 32-year-old son, died in 1989 from thyroid cancer. As I touch the stone, I feel connected to Dave and to the place that stone came from.

In 1979 Dave felt a lump in his throat while shaving one morning. Doctors found a huge malignant tumor. It was surgically removed. In spite of that, the cancer did metastasize to various other locations, the gravest of which was the cervical area of his spine. That area was then radiated to the limit. The radiation reduced the tumor mass dramatically, but not completely. It grew back during the next two years; however, it was not treatable because the area could not tolerate any further radiation. An attempt at chemotherapy was unsuccessful and surgery was out of the question because the tumor was so thoroughly integrated with his vertebrae. That's when the increasing paralysis came into play. A halo brace was necessary the final seven months of his life because the tumor had structurally weakened his spine, making it impossible for him to hold his head up unassisted.

My wife went to live with him so that he was able to be at home instead of a care institute, and we had wonderful people in to help. I flew to Seattle from Philadelphia every two weeks for a long weekend. Fortunately, I had a job that allowed the ease of working in both places and a wonderful boss who made it happen.

When we first found out about the cancer, we didn't believe for a minute it would kill him. We thought there was a solution, and we'd find it and lick it. Those first eight years he led an outwardly normal life most of the time, but we were increasingly aware this disease wasn't going to go away.

Family life was stressful during this time. You have an increasingly sobering, scary thing thrust into your family, and at times things could be tense. I had another world at work; Sue worked at home, alone, and our minds were in different places when I would come home at the end of the day or at the end of a business trip. Dave and his illness were on her mind more than they were on mine, and that was sometimes a source of stress between us and a source of guilt for me. After Dave died we learned we had to tolerate the differences in grieving. For example, one partner may not be able to stand any pictures around the house; the other can't get enough of them to look at. You have to learn to be tolerant and understanding of each other.

Because of the quality home health care we had for Dave that last year, we set up a fund for professional development in his honor and named for him. Family and friends donated money in his memory. The fund allows the staff at the care center to go on retreats or learn more in the technical video training series, for example, all of which provides better care for the patients.

After Dave died we found friends who were helpful were the ones who weren't afraid of us. One man I knew somewhat, who worked with a competitive firm, interrupted a business trip to come to Dave's funeral in Seattle. He brought a tray of food, plopped down on our couch and became part of the family. Another person sent me a 'stupid' greeting card with an old time photo of the Keystone Cops on a hand train. He wrote on it "Got this ridiculous card because what has happened is so ridiculous, I can't contemplate it." That was a really helpful expression for him to make. To this day I get choked up thinking about it.

A couple we were friendly with came over and sat with us. I remember she said, "I can't imagine how difficult this is. Tell me about Dave and his death." All these people and others led us into what we needed to do, talk and cry about it. They are still very good friends to this day.

Others were anxious for our grieving to be over. These people don't have a clue how this all works. Some avoided us. It was not painful, but noticeable. Our attitude was "That's their problem."

When Dave died, Sue, our daughter Karen who was two years younger, and I were with him. Being able to hold his hand when he died was the most important, meaningful thing I've ever done in my life. The three of us who remained were in it together and pledged to be supportive and help each other to get through this.

Dave had worked for Boeing and told us to take the insurance money he was due and have a family reunion in Hawaii with all the cousins, aunts, uncles and grandparents. Among other things, we were to celebrate his life. From May, when he died, until that Thanksgiving, we focused on just that. Sue took care of all the arrangements. Twenty-two of us went for a week. The three of us went two days earlier to scatter some of his ashes on Kauai, a place he loved.

Men do grieve differently than women, but I have to generalize more broadly than that and say "people" on the whole grieve differently.

For me reading was helpful. I didn't want to read stories about people; I wanted expert opinions about how this would play out. I tried reading, ***Lament for a Son,*** which was too painful. I needed objective opinions to give me some direction. One book, ***Beyond Endurance,*** had a chart that compared the intensity of different aspects of grief experiences for parents whose child died of cancer compared to a child who died unexpectedly. It helped me say, 'Oh, this is how it will go, the ups and downs.' It was a two-year course for me plotted there. I don't think this is what the author intended, but it worked for me.

With nothing to focus on months after the reunion, we became devastated and drained. We sought out the local chapter of The Compassionate Friends who were a tremendous help. For the four years we were active in Valley Forge, Pennsylvania, we saw the chapter grow in numbers from 40-100 members. We met every two weeks. It was a time that I could always devote to 'Dave' thoughts and conversation. It let me put aside the work week and think about him. For the first six months I couldn't talk at all. If I opened my mouth, my throat would close. At first it was just thinking and being with people; before and after meetings I could stand around and talk. That wasn't a problem. Finally, in my own time, I was able to open up. We keep in contact with many of these people.

I am active, as is my wife, in the national Compassionate Friends organization to this day, even after moving to Tucson, Arizona. It is like a family reunion at the national conventions. Our daughter, Karen, also got active with the national office. Karen was appointed to the TCF National Board of Directors, where she served for four years, two as president. She was the first sibling to serve as president of the board. Sue and I were committed to helping and working on various committees also. One year, because of some special needs in the national office, we spent a week each month in Oak Brook, Illinois, working 60 hours a week helping out wherever we could. This organization had been a great value to us, and we wanted to give back to it.

In Tucson we also got very active in a very small chapter which grew a lot in numbers over the years. We are now active in helping to promote the recognition in this country of The Compassionate Friends

Worldwide Candle Lighting the second Sunday in December at 7 p.m. in every time zone around the world. It is in honor of all children who have died. We distribute buttons of this event, designed by the organization, to chapters across the United States. TCF now has 600 chapters, so this is a big job.

Three years ago my daughter saw an on-line bereavement grant offer that could be used for leadership training in various chapters of TCF. We applied and got a $100,000 grant. Sue and I were part of the committee that wrote the grant request and designed the Chapter Leadership Training Program, and we were part of the faculty team that conducted the workshop in fourteen locations around the country over an 18-month period. The program taught basic TCF chapter leadership skills and reached over 550 chapter leadership people from approximately 275 chapters.

Most recently, the three of us were involved with a private research study conducted by NFO Research, Inc. on behalf of TCF. The research company sent out 20,000 questionnaires to get a cross section of the general population in order to understand the scope of its mission. Results show that 19 percent of adults have experienced the death of a child, any age, any cause. Other results stated that approximately one million children die each year from the following breakdown: miscarriage (43%), illness (27%), accident (13%) and stillbirth (11%).

One area of the survey I found extremely interesting was in the telephone calls to bereaved parents. Statistical results showed 72% are still married to the same person. Of the remaining 28%, 16% were widowed. Only 12% were actually divorced, and even among the 12%, only one out of four felt that the impact of the death of their child contributed to the divorce. These numbers show that the often claimed divorce rate of 70-80% is not true. When your child dies you don't need the additional burden of hearing that your marriage will probably be in trouble. This part of the survey should be comforting to many.

Everything we do with TCF is a tribute to Dave. He was a straight A student and stickler for details and perfection. We are strongly influenced by that in our work for the organization. We want it to be quality.

As Sue and I continue to travel, if we find a special place, we take some of Dave's ashes and scatter them. In that way he is always with us on our journeys. If I forget the ashes, there is always the stone I pick up to add to my collection. I touch it…and smile.

Observations of Karl

It is obvious that Karl's work with The Compassionate Friends, as well as his family's, was critical in helping the family move on with their lives, while honoring Dave's life with the work they did and still do. Karl seems well aware that there is no one right thing to do when a child dies, nor is there one right organization for everyone. We do know from the survey that less than half the population which could benefit from parental grief support organizations even know that such organizations exist. National visibility is the key, so the newly bereaved know they exist. Many organizations are very specific; there are some for suicide, SIDS, AIDS and others for alcohol and drugs. Additional ones can be found in church organizations, Hospice groups and hospitals. Professionals also know of many of these groups and can direct you.

Karl and his family were also fortunate with the support they received from friends and family. Knowing someone cares about you can ease your awful pain. In the research survey, over 80% of parents said that family and friends were the most helpful, followed by co-workers and clergy.

Karl talked about reading books so that he knew what to expect. The survey showed that women were more likely to read while men were more likely to reach out to funeral homes/directors.

His employer was helpful in allowing him flexible working hours so that he could visit his son 2,500 miles away those last seven months. Sixty-nine percent of those surveyed said their employer was "very" or "somewhat" helpful with flexible schedules and in conveying compassion verbally and through cards and flowers.

Karl is likely to always be an involved, passionate person, who says, "You want me to tell you all the things I'm doing with The Compassionate Friends and others? How much time do you have?"

4

Jennafer

"I became involved with the Victim's Impact Panel where part of the criminal's retribution is to listen to parents' stories...They begin to understand my loss..."

Celeste

If I can get one person to listen to me about not drinking and driving, then I have made a difference. I can't bring Jennafer back, but I can honor her memory.

My 15-year-old daughter was killed by a drunk driver who, through a plea bargain, will serve six years behind bars and four years probation. She should have been in for life. It wasn't her first drunk driving offense.

Jennafer was a very independent child. She always stretched her limits with me, particularly where her boyfriend was concerned and what time she had to be in from a date. In spite of that, we did get along well. Thanksgiving of 1993 I went with my future husband to Utah to visit his relatives. Because I couldn't afford to take my two daughters, Jennafer and Carrie, age 13, and they did not want to drive that far, they stayed with my mother. The whole plane ride my stomach hurt like something was wrong. It continued through the night. On Thanksgiving morning at 6 a.m. I received a call saying that Jennafer was dead. I started screaming. I was hysterical. It was not possible. Less than 24 hours earlier I had kissed both daughters good-bye. A car accident, I was told, but knew nothing more. Anxiety attacks assailed me on the trip home. We had to stop for medicine to calm me down.

I learned that a drunk woman went through a red light and smashed into the passenger side of the car where Jennafer was sitting on her way home from a date. She died hours later at the hospital on the operating table. They tried desperately to save her, but to no avail. Her boyfriend was not injured seriously. I never got to say good-bye, and it still hurts. I had to call a funeral home to open on Thanksgiving Day to pick up her body, and never saw her until she was at the funeral home.

My friends at work were very supportive. They helped defray the cost of the funeral expenses by getting hot dogs, buns and Pepsi donated, which in turn were sold to raise money for the cremation. I keep the vase in the house and sometimes find myself taking down the vase from a shelf when I am depressed and want to talk to Jennafer.

I was still in an unbelievable daze during those first few weeks and ended up actually shutting down for about a year. Cooking and cleaning were out of the question. A week after the funeral I returned to work but found myself just wandering around. I had the type of job, a back-up scanning coordinator for Smith's food store, where I had to motivate myself, and it was impossible to get motivated.

They never took me off the position, but I worked 2-days a week in the check-out area. When a customer would come through with alcohol, I wanted to throw it at them. I was very sensitive about it. I carded everyone. I didn't care how old they were. Late at night if a customer came in drunk and wanted to buy more alcohol, I would find myself getting into fights with them when they realized I wouldn't sell the alcohol to them.

At home I would walk by Jennafer's room, memories would trigger my mind, and I would find myself standing there screaming. I didn't touch her room for the entire time I lived in that house, almost a year. Everything was left just as it was that November day. I had already bought her Christmas presents but could not return them. I opened them and placed the items around the room she kept spotless. When my eyes see the 1993 calendar on her wall, time stops, I wish the years away, and I see Jennafer blotting her lipstick on each calendar day, a personal touch to mark it off.

To this day Carrie has never come to terms with Jennafer's death. She blames herself because they had a fight that last night and Carrie, in her anger, had wished Jennafer dead. Jennafer, most times would have risen to the occasion but this time did not, had hugged Carrie and told her before leaving on her date, "You don't mean that, and I love you very much; give me a hug." Carrie won't talk about her sister very much except to her son Austin. I wish she would. I'd like to share our mutual memories. Carrie is now married and does tell her own child about his aunt, so I know she remembers with love.

Suicidal thoughts ran through my mind at the beginning, but because of Carrie, I knew I had to keep going for her. I was in grief therapy for years. At first it was not helpful, but later on that changed.

Because my current husband is not Jennafer's natural father, it is difficult to talk to him about her. He and Jennafer did not get along because she felt her time with me was taken away by his presence. But he has been wonderful with me since her death, taken care of me through the worst times, cooked all the meals and helped with Carrie. We married the year after Jennafer died. If a couple can survive the death of a child, whether the child is both of yours or not, it makes the marriage stronger. It bonds you in a way nothing else can. For me, it was part of what saved my life.

Jennafer's real father, who lives in the same city as we do, only came to the funeral. He had not seen the girls very much in those eight years after the divorce. He told Carrie at the funeral that after he dealt with

Jennafer's death he would be in Carrie's life forever. She has never heard from him since that day.

Five days after Jennafer died I went to her school. I wanted to clean out her locker myself. I didn't want school officials to do it for me. It was too personal. While there I got in touch with the SADD director and asked what I could do to preserve her memory. A tree was planted. The director then asked me months later to speak at the mock car crash SADD puts on at the school each spring before prom and graduation to bring home the reality of the consequences of drinking and driving. I agreed to do it so I could talk about my daughter. I'm a very emotional person and to this day still have trouble talking about the accident. The news media interviewed me at home to tie it into the mock crash and, since then, there have been many follow-up news articles. The media continues to use my high profile story year after year with different angles related to the impact Jennafer's death has had on me.

From SADD I began working with MADD, spoke at boys' and girls' clubs, at many schools and at the police department. What I say to the kids is "You have a right to say no. You don't have to get in that car to go home if you think the driver is impaired. Call your parents. Call a cab. It's not worth your life." Sometimes I have them do an exercise where they close their eyes and think of someone they really care about who has moved away. "You can still call and talk to them. How would you feel if you were cut off from them forever? That's the position I'm in and will be in the rest of my life." It brings the point home.

Through the Phoenix and Mesa police departments and MADD, I then became involved with the Victim's Impact Panel. The court system makes this a mandatory part of a sentence. Part of the criminal's retribution is to listen to parent's stories. It affects some people. They begin to understand my loss. They come up to me afterwards and say how sorry they are. You can see that you've touched them. Others are not at all interested. Some laugh. I say to them, "What is so funny about death?" or "If you had used your brain and called a taxi, you wouldn't have to listen to me now." Others I have asked to take their walkman and the earphones off. A few get angry. Why don't you get on with your life?" they say to me. They don't understand I have gotten on with my life. If I hadn't, I'd be sitting home in a corner. Doing this work is how I am dealing with the rest of my life.

Both Carrie and my husband have spoken to groups also. My husband speaks about what a husband can do to help a person through this who is not the natural father. He doesn't like to speak, but with a little persuasion, he does. He was very influential in giving me a kick and getting me started on the speaking circuit. Carrie is uncomfortable with it.

Since Jennafer died on Thanksgiving, I don't celebrate that holiday any more. As the day approaches I become a basket case. I want to be left alone during this time, so if my husband wants to see his family, he understands that I just can't go. He also understands that when I snap at him, I don't really mean it. It's my sensitivity at this time of year. Each year I get a little better, but for now it's still there. Christmas was Jennifer's favorite time of the year. She loved decorating the tree. I have a hard time decorating the house and Carrie won't help me.

For five years I went to the crash site three times a year: her birthday, Christmas season and the day she died, since there was no grave to go to. After getting permission from the city I put up a cross marking the site. I would go there, stand on the corner and cry. My husband and Carrie finally convinced me that it wasn't necessary to go. But vandals continuously tore the cross down until this last year when I cemented a steel one into the ground and put a bird of paradise around it. That was Jennafer's favorite flower. The kind lady who lives next door waters the flowers during the year for me, and so far it is still intact. Now I only go when I'm on that side of town and bring either fresh flowers or a candle.

Candles were another thing my daughter loved. I light them at home on the anniversary of her death each year and on the Jewish holiday of Yom Kippur.

A special remembrance of Jennafer is my license plate with her name on it and around the rim "In Memory of Jennafer" with her birth and death date. I don't want her to be forgotten. I want her name everywhere, and when I can afford it, I will build many memorials in her honor.

On Jennafer's sixth anniversary of her death, Carrie asked that I try to celebrate Thanksgiving for my new grandson. It was his first Thanksgiving. I did, and all went well.

Observations of Celeste

Celeste is often brought to tears as she speaks of Jennafer. It does not embarrass her to cry. She just finds it difficult when she thinks of what a senseless waste of a human life this was. And so avoidable. That is one reason she talks to groups, hoping they will see the importance of being responsible drivers. The other reason is to simply talk about her daughter and how much Jennafer meant to her.

SADD is the national organization for high school students that creates programs to deal with serious issues young adults are facing today, two of which are drunk driving and underage drinking. MADD also has the same goals and in addition deals with victim support. Recent statistics from the National Highway Traffic Safety Administration estimate that 39 percent of all fatal U.S. crashes involve alcohol. A majority of drivers who cause these accidents are between 25-44 years old. The hours that most accidents occur are between 5 p.m. and 1 a.m. Jennafer's case falls right into these statistics.

Celeste would like to help reduce these numbers so others will not have to go through what she has endured. She believes only education on the consequences of driving drunk can do that. For now Celeste says she will continue to talk about Jennafer to these organizations she has been involved with and to anyone out there who will listen. "I have a big mouth," she says, "but a lot to say!"

5

Stephanie and Stephen

"Grief is a selfish emotion. I realized that I couldn't expect we would be grieving identically or that my husband could fix the unfixable... We were blessed with the greatest gift of all, the chance to love and be loved by children again..."

Pat and Wayne

After both our children died we had a tough decision to make. Should we have more? Pat and I know we made the right decision for us, but every couple facing this situation has to decide what is right for them...Wayne

Our two children, Stephanie, 8, and Stephen, 5, were both killed in 1991. The kids and I were on our way home one evening. As I sat waiting to turn onto my street a racing design motorcycle sped past me. I looked down the street, saw two more motorcycles a considerable distance away and proceeded to make the turn. I glanced down the street again and realized that the motorcycles were speeding up. I'm unsure if my next words were out loud or in my head, but the words were "My God! They're speeding up!" Then I felt the impact. One of them hit the passenger side of the car where my children were sitting. I remember screaming, "My babies, my babies!" It never entered my thought process that either one of them could die. I knew they were injured and needed help, but die—NEVER! Today, in my mind I can clearly see Stephanie lying there, but I can't see Stephen. I can feel myself turning around in the seat to check on him and then I see nothing. I've since concluded that when I turned around, Stephen was already dead, and I knew it, but my brain just wouldn't process it...Pat

I received a call at my store from a neighbor who I had never met. He told me there had been an accident, and I should come home. When I quizzed him to find out if the accident was serious, he asked me point blank, "Do you have children?" When I responded positively, he said, "Then you'd better get home now!" When I arrived at the scene, I found the streets blocked off. Pat's car sat in the wrong side of the road, the passenger side crumpled. They had already been taken to the hospital, only a block away. His calmness led me to believe everyone was fine. At the hospital I was led to Pat who was being treated in the emergency room. Grabbing my shirt she screamed "How are the kids?" After checking, I told her the doctors were working on them. I was led to the hospital's family waiting room where I found family and friends already arriving. Within an hour a doctor came in and said Stephanie had stabilized but Stephen didn't make it. I stood in shock trying to grasp her words as I heard the quiet erupt into wails of grief. I told Pat a few minutes later...Wayne

It was hard to process what Wayne was saying. What was happening and what he was saying were not real. They were just words at that moment. I was crying, but no tears came out. I fought hard to maintain some kind of control over the situation, the children and myself, but the hospital just kept trying to sedate me...Pat

Still worried about Pat, I was then asked if I wanted to see Stephen. I did. I remember a nurse taking one arm and a friend the other, supporting me. My legs were useless. I could only take baby steps down that seemingly endless corridor. We reached a door, which swung open, and I spotted my little Stephen lying on this big table. I was helped to him and was left alone. A tube was still in his mouth. He could have been asleep. But I watched his chest and it did not move. A few scratches on his face were the only visible scars from his ordeal. I stroked his cheek and whispered quietly in his ear, "I love you and I will never forget you." I was told I'd have to hurry if I wanted to see Stephanie. She was being readied to be flown by helicopter to Children's Hospital and time was critical. Though Stephanie was unconscious when I saw her, I whispered words of encouragement. "I love you" were my last words to her as she was loaded into the helicopter...Wayne

I agonized after the accident that I didn't get to see my son. I understood and could reason through that Stephanie had to very quickly be moved to another hospital and, therefore, there wasn't time to allow me to see her. But Stephen and I were in the same hospital. For a long time I felt that I was a bad mother because I didn't ask to see him. It took a lot of therapy sessions to realize that it would have been prudent and compassionate for the hospital to ask me. I was a stranger, alone and frightened on this grief walk. I needed someone's guidance and understanding. I really think the hospital should have been attuned to that...Pat

I was driven to Children's Hospital where doctors were warming up Stephanie's body slowly in hopes that brain activity would return. When I saw her, I couldn't believe the change. She was so swollen because of all the intravenous liquids given to her. As my tears dropped to the floor, I pulled a picture of Stephanie in her silver dance recital outfit from my wallet and handed it to the nurses. "I just want you to know who you are working on," I told them, sobbing. At 2 a.m. the doctors told me what I had feared. Her body had been warmed. Tests had been run. There was no brain activity. I was asked to consider organ donation. I called Pat at the other hospital and told her Stef was dead. We discussed that she was such a loving child, we were certain she would want her organs donated to help others. We believe that one or two children may be alive today because of her donation...Wayne

Pat and I went through a lot of professional therapy that first year and that helped. I also sent letters and cards to people whose child had died. I needed to connect with people in a similar situation. I would get the names from the daily newspaper and tell them this had happened to us and said we were thinking about them. I did this for a couple of years and occasionally, I received a letter back thanking me, and it made me feel good that I could help them in some small way. We even met one of the couples a few years later. They said I probably wouldn't remember them, but they spoke of how much they were touched by my letter…Wayne

The Compassionate Friends was a life saver. We joined a chapter 20 miles away and at first I didn't want to go. "Take me anyplace but there," I would tell Wayne. I felt that there wasn't a person on this earth who could hurt as badly as I did or could possibly understand how I felt. Then one day one of the moms started talking about the videotape that never switched off in her head. My ears perked up, and I thought, 'My goodness!' That's happening to someone else too?' As I listened I realized the people sitting around the table really did understand. We had some of the same demons. I knew I was in the right place…Pat

The meetings were great because I got to hear others' responses. Sometimes we would break up into groups, and sometimes Pat and I would go to different tables and share separately. No two people grieve alike, and we were no exception. In these groups I could speak candidly and sometimes say things I wasn't comfortable telling even Pat…Wayne

I wanted Wayne to fix the situation, fix my broken heart and make everything normal again. After all, over the years I was programmed and grew to expect that was his role. When something needed to be fixed, I went to him. But one day Wayne turned to me and said, "You know, it's hard for me to throw you a lifeline when I'm drowning myself." Those words were a real turning point. Grief is a selfish emotion. I realized then that I couldn't expect we would be grieving identically or that he could fix the unfixable. Those words turned things around and brought us closer together during this process…Pat

From the TCF group Wayne and I attended we started a satellite chapter in 1993 closer to our home and became chapter leaders and newsletter editors which we continue to do today. Then, in 1995 we were asked to take over producing the two newsletters, one for bereaved parents, the other for bereaved siblings for the national organization of Compassionate Friends. Wayne has a journalism background and enjoys writing and editing, and I enjoy doing the layout and design. A few years ago we combined the two national newsletters into a magazine for bereaved families following the death of a child. Working on those publications has been a rewarding experience for both of us…Pat

The holiday season was really difficult for Wayne and I. When Stef and Steve were alive we made Christmas a really big deal. It was unthinkable to celebrate Christmas and put up a tree without them. Then the third year after they died I had an idea: since we certainly couldn't celebrate Christmas as if they had never existed, why not decorate the house with their love. We wrote a letter to friends and family explaining what a difficult step this was to take and asked them to send us something to hang on the tree in remembrance of Stephanie and Stephen. We got a great response. One of the many remembrances sent that is very dear to us is a small tap shoe from Stephanie's dance instructor. The special remembrances made the holidays so much easier…Pat

What really helped Wayne and I most to cope with our loss was having more children. Christopher was born in August, 1992, and Katherine "Katie" in October, 1993. Because of medical reasons, we weren't sure we'd be able to have more children and were as shocked as the doctors when it happened! Perhaps helping to cope with a death of a child is the wrong reason to have subsequent children, but in our situation, we woke up one morning still feeling we were parents but not having anyone to parent. It was a lonely, awful feeling. There was a tremendous void which needed to be filled and a lot of love to give…Pat

I have to admit that when Chris and Katie were born I was almost afraid to love them too much, afraid to hurt again like I had before, if anything were to happen to them. And I felt guilty that the world was viewing them as replacements, and since they had arrived Wayne and I were "over" Stef and Steve's death. When I would say "I love you" to Chris or Katie, I would always softly say, "and I love you, Stef and Steve." I wanted Stephanie and Stephen to realize I still loved them and these new children did not replace them...Pat

Pat and I talked about it a great deal before we had more children. We would say, "Is it worth taking the chance of losing another child?" But we knew we had an abundance of love in us to give to other children. We went ahead knowing we were taking a chance there could be more heartache in the future. It was our decision. This doesn't mean it's right for everyone, and each person must make his own decision. But we haven't regretted it one moment...Wayne

Chris and Katie know about Stephen and Stephanie and that they are part of our family. Wayne and I talk about Stephanie and Stephen all the time with them. When Stef or Steve's birthday comes around, it's not unusual for Chris and Katie to ask us to make a cake for them. And we always light candles on special anniversaries, birthdays and holidays. Our mantel is full of candles...Pat

From our experience we lost many friends. I think we represented their worst nightmares. They didn't know what to say to us, so it was easier to stay away. They still saw themselves as parents, but to them we were not. When I got pregnant, they made assumptions we had healed, and everything was now okay with us. They didn't understand...Pat

To me it seems God played a real role in helping us to survive. He blessed us with the greatest gift of all, the chance to love and be loved by children again. And, in those darkest moments all bereaved parents experience, something has always come along at the right time to help such as being asked to edit the TCF national newsletters, interviewing the creator of Precious Moments, Sam Butcher, a fellow bereaved parent; and I had some dreams that were so real, I knew I saw Stephanie and Stephen, and they were telling me they were fine. That was God's way of comforting me in a way nothing else could...Wayne

Observations of Pat and Wayne

If you lose all your children but are fortunate enough to have others as Pat and Wayne were, that does not mean you are replacing the ones lost. Having more children is a very personal decision. It should be talked about and considered carefully before any commitments are made. What is right for one couple can be devastating for another.

To hold a marriage together is not a reason couples should have additional children. A good marriage full of love and the ability to understand and accept each other's differences will survive most anything, even death. If the marriage breaks up, there was probably something else wrong with it all along. Bringing new children into a troubled marriage does not solve the problems. It only creates new ones for both the couple and the subsequent children. An important thing to remember is if a couple has, as Wayne says, "an abundance of love" in them to share with additional children and realizes each child is his own person, their lives will be enriched by that child's presence.

Organ donation is one way to help save lives. When a family member dies, sparing others that same grief can become important. Pat and Wayne felt if they could save someone's life with Stephanie's organs, it was the right choice to make. There are many others who, by their wills, on their driver's licenses, or through conversations with loved ones, choose to make that same life-altering decision.

Their work with The Compassionate Friends, their journalistic endeavors at producing newsletters and a national magazine and their Christian upbringing have all played a part in Pat and Wayne's ability to heal. As Wayne points out, "It does get easier with time."

6

Sheryl

> *"When my daughter died I felt like I was in the bottom of a slimy pit, trying to claw my way to the top and always slipping back. Finally, I went to see a psychiatrist and with a combination of medicine and therapy was brought out of serious depression..."*
>
> Helene

What has helped me heal the most is knowing that through my daughter's death, many lives have been saved.

In 1982 not much was known as to why children, teens and adults were dying from a common ailment, the stomach flu. This is how Sheryl, my 26-year-old daughter, died. The autopsy, finally released after repeated requests, said the coroner could not find a cause. To me that was unacceptable. I had to know why.

My daughter, who was living with us at the time, became very sick with vomiting and diarrhea. I was frightened by her extreme illness and took her to the doctor after the second day. We left the doctor's office with instructions for her to drink gatorade. She died thirty minutes later. I tried CPR but could not revive her. She had been frequently ill since puberty with various illnesses. She was highly allergic and seemed to have a weakened immune system.

An autopsy was done, but the results were not released. I searched and found other cases similar to my daughter's. I knew there must be a connection but was having trouble finding additional leads. My husband at the time, Burt, told me to let it go. He could not deal with the death and certainly was not interested in pursuing an autopsy report. I relented and let it be.

Burt was able to express some of what he felt at the time when he wrote a sympathy letter to a colleague at work whose son died right after Sheryl. I kept the letter since it said more to me about my husband's feelings than anything he could ever express to me. Some of these passages follow. *"As you will readily find out, the most meaningful thing anyone can say to you at this time is just 'I'm terribly sorry.' No other words or thoughts can begin to console you. Your life has changed; you will now start to feel the shock, the feelings of guilt, the asking 'why', the frustration and the protest. There are only a small group of us that know what you are feeling at this time.Your friends and relatives may tell you they know how you feel, but you as parents know only too well that they really don't. Check out your local chapter of The Compassionate Friends. As hard as it will be, call them and try to attend one of their monthly meetings. Right now you are probably surrounded by family and friends and at no time in your life have you ever needed support from others as you do right now. That's good. Lean on them, but later on you'll find that they will shy away from talking about the death of your son. They will be afraid to mention it for fear of upsetting you. And you will shy away from too much dwelling on the subject because you'll realize that everyone except you has gone back to being occupied with his own problems even though they seem insignificant to you.*

"We have found through this group that we have a place to talk to people who are genuinely concerned, that do understand because it is a group of parents all of whom have had a child die. It has helped Helene and I.

You'll notice I said 'have had a child die.' That's another thing you'll find: people will use all types of phrases except that one. And yet, I believe as a surviving parent we must say it, just like that. Using other words doesn't make it any easier or any less true. My wife and I are there if you want to talk. And that's important, too. Whatever you do, keep talking to each other. For the next few months you'll find it harder to help each other than ever before because you are both in need of support as compared to one of you going through a crisis where the other can be helpful. Lastly, read some grief books written by those who have gone through the experience. These authors have been able to put into words what we all feel."

When my husband died from a heart attack eight months later, I was back at the coroner's door. My husband died of a broken heart; I know it. He could never accept Sheryl's death or come to terms with it, even though he tried very hard. After sending letters to the county board of supervisors, my lawyer and the medical staff of the hospital, the inconclusive autopsy results on Sheryl were released.

I contacted a Dr. Martin Blaser, chief of the infectious disease section at the Veterans Administration Medical Center in Denver, where I lived at the time. He was a top authority on intestinal problems. After further research he called and told me I was right. It was something specific. Sheryl had died of a bacteria called Campylobacter jejuni, found most commonly in undercooked chicken. According to Dr. Blaser, this type of diarrhea can be life-threatening, but at the time most doctors did not know about it. Sheryl's story became the focus of TV, magazine and medical journal reports that to this day have been credited with saving many lives. Cooking meat, poultry and fish correctly, washing these products, and cleaning up counters after use have kept millions from serious consequences. Her death has helped others live. At least her life wasn't wasted.

One of my closest friends said Sheryl lived life as if she knew she wouldn't live long. She was enthusiastic, never complained and had a tremendous zest for living. Guitar music was her main focus.

Every year she would miss up to 1/2 of the entire school year. Her five foot frame could not deal with all the sickness. Even her thyroid gland died. When she became an adult, I never knew she was a research patient at the University of Iowa because of her thyroid and severe fluid retention problems until I read about her condition in some medical journals.

I have come a long way these last 17 years. I went into total shock when Sheryl died. We were very close. To this day I have lost a lot of my memory. Entire portions of my life are lost. I believe the cause was my daughter's death and subsequently my husband's death so shortly after. My therapist explained the mind can block memories as a way of coping after extreme shocks.

A teacher by profession, I eventually gave that up. When my daughter died I was an ad sales manager. There were days I would have an appointment, start to drive to the meeting but eventually turn around because I was not up to facing anyone for any reason.

The first six months I was in such shock that when I was able to work, it was like being a robot. I had no feelings. I couldn't deal head on with anything. I would even go to a grocery store, walk in, couldn't remember why I was there, turn around and walk out.

I felt like I was in the bottom of a slimy pit, trying to claw my way to the top and always slipping back. Finally, I went to see a psychiatrist. It took him four months to break down the barriers I had set up as protection against everyone and everything. I was in a deep depression from the shock of both deaths so close together.

With a combination of medicine and therapy, the doctor brought me out of this serious depression. I recently read a medical article which said that a combination of medicine and therapy helps 85 percent of those depressed, whereas medicine alone, only 52 percent and therapy alone, only 55 percent.

I have cousins in Canada. When I visited them after my daughter died, they talked a lot about their grandmother who was widowed and came alone from Russia, making a life for herself and her children. She started with a grocery cart and eventually built the store, building and apartment above. She was a successful grocery store owner and the breadwinner of her family. Through my sorrow I listened with great interest, pride and love. And I realized if that's the kind of stock I come from and she could do all that, then I could survive too. It was one of the incidents that really helped me move forward.

But at the beginning I could not sleep at all and even thought of suicide. One grief book, ***The Bereaved Parent*** by Harriet Schiff said, "You're either suicidal or not. Decide and find a way to live or get it over with." I finally had my first full night of sleep after reading that. I then read Rabbi Kushner's book ***When Bad Things Happen To Good People*** and realized God can not control everything. Acts of God are the goodness and kindness of people around you that help you heal, your support system.

Reading everything I could get my hands on was another factor I believe contributed most to my healing. In 1982 there were not many grief books, but I read all I could find. Then I even turned to reading medical books, getting statistics on various illnesses and learning about stress and how to handle it. When you read the grief books, you find the feelings you can't voice are there. It is comforting to me, as it was to my step-daughters who lost their mother at a young age.

The Compassionate Friends group in the Denver area were also wonderful. In one grief group session, paper plates were sectioned off. Sections included how much of your life was your career, how much was family, how much was children, how much your husband, etc. Then we drew lines and cut out the section or sections that were now gone from our lives. In my case 50 percent was gone. We were told we now had to find a way to fill that portion of our life again. It was a very graphic way to see reality and what had happened in my life.

I remember once having a psychologist speak to the group whose main emphasis was grief counseling, and ironically, a few months later she, too, was mourning the death of her own child. This counselor thought she had the answers, but only when it happens to you personally does it all make sense. Everybody grieves differently, and I found the methods used in this group just right for me.

For the first eight months I went to the cemetery every day in Denver. Now that I no longer live there, I rarely have the chance to go. My friends, though, bring flowers and keep the grave clean. When visiting Colorado, I choose to go to the memorial pavilion in Elbert.

At a summer camp in Elbert, Colorado, my first husband and I started to build this memorial pavilion in our daughter's memory. When my husband died I completed it in both of their memories. Money was raised by family and friends through performing a benefit concert and donations. My husband's company matched funds. It is a fitting tribute to my daughter and her love of music. It is used year round as a meeting and entertainment pavilion.

Eventually, I became reacquainted with my high school sweetheart who I married. I can talk to my second husband about anything, but he can never really understand what I am going through and he knows that.

My life is very different now; we have moved and made new friends. It took me a while to understand that my good friends today did not know Sheryl, so while they can empathize with me, it is still very difficult for them to relate to her death. So, I don't talk much about her in my everyday life though she's never out of my mind.

On the other hand, my close friends from my younger days in Denver and Chicago are still extremely supportive. One, whose son was named after my daughter and husband, keeps a scrapbook of the history of the two families so the son will always know where he came from, who his mom's friends were and who he was named after. His legacy will be kept intact.

Exercise is very important to me in this new life. Without exercise (treadmill, tennis, or walking), I wouldn't be able to function each day. It is essential to my well-being and keeps me from being depressed. I am an avid tennis player.

One thing I try to do in my spare time is talk to those who have lost a child. I know through my experience I can relate on the deepest level. Nobody who has not lost a child can understand on that level. I show them I survived the nightmare. By helping others, you help yourself.

Observations of Helene…

Helene is one parent who could not have survived her ordeal without some type of therapy. She believes it helped her tremendously even though a partial memory loss still haunts her today. I could see as we sat across the table from each other how frustrated she would get when she couldn't remember a name or a place or an entire situation dealing directly with her daughter. Sometimes, a portion of it would surface, but most of the time she just apologized for the memory loss.

Helen's statement about "being in the bottom of a slimy pit trying to get out but always slipping back" is a perfect description of what many parents go through. We have a bad day, and then we have some good days when we think our lives are getting better. One small comment can trigger our grief again. It could be a poem, a special date, or someone just saying the child's name. Suddenly, we are back to Point A again and hoping the next day will be better. It is a pattern that can repeat itself for years. Sometimes we can get out of that pit ourselves, sometimes, as in Helene's case, counseling helped.

Counseling is a viable alternative. Parents need to try everything possible to heal, and if a kind doctor or compassionate counselor can show that there is a section of that slimy pit with a few ridges, then the climb out can begin.

It was easy to see as I talked to Helene that here was a woman eager to continue to live a good, healthy life full of friends, exercise, reading and talking to others who have lost a child, but never forgetting as she walks into the memorial pavilion in Colorado, one of her proudest accomplishments, her daughter Sheryl.

7

Craig

"I now work for the Mental Health Association of Arizona in public speaking and education. In a program called "Options," we can go into the high schools and educate teachers and students on the symptoms of depression to avoid suicide. I do this because I won't be part of the shame attached to mental illness..."

Nancy

It was little things happening that alerted me something was very wrong. But still, as a mother, I didn't want to acknowledge something could be wrong with my son. Craig was 21 years old when he put a gun to his head and ended his life in 1990.

My popular, affectionate son, involved in sports and many school activities, became a loner after his first year of college, began to hear voices by the second year and found it difficult to concentrate by the third year. In his second year of college we began to see a series of therapists, and he eventually spent some time at mental hospitals. One therapist thought he might be bipolar, another said he had childhood issues with some children that needed resolving. Not one diagnosed the real problem.

Craig, diagnosing himself, thought he was schizophrenic. The psychologists laughed at him. Two days before his death he saw a new psychologist who did confirm what we suspected. For the next 30 hours Craig didn't say anything and didn't eat. He then got in his car at the house, put on a Grateful Dead tape and shot himself to death.

I was at a luncheon that day and was taken back to the office where I found my daughter, Lois, five years older than Craig, and the therapist, who told me what had happened.

The gun was bought in a gun shop. Mentally ill people shouldn't be allowed to purchase guns. They aren't able to be responsible. What I've learned since then is that if someone wants to kill himself, they will find a way, gun or not.

"No," I screamed. "It can't be." Not one doctor in the three years had said he was suicidal. I went to the hospital to see his body. I still thought it was a mistake. Police told me not to go in. "That's my son," I said. "I'm going in." He was cleaned up from the bullet wound, covered up to his head with a sheet. I took the sheet down to see what he was wearing. He always wore an army fatigue jacket for a sense of security. Because the jacket was not on, it told me he was at peace with his decision. He had found a way to convince himself it was the right thing to do. When I saw where the bullet went in on the side of his head, I finally realized he was dead. I held him. "It's okay," I said. "You're going to a better place where you won't hurt anymore."

The police came back to the house with me to check for notes. Suicide is against the law, and they needed to see if Craig had left anything. He hadn't.

My son, in the last few years, had listened to tapes and watched TV at the same time to drown out the voices he heard in his head. He had thrown them out the night before he died. I guess he knew he wouldn't need them. There would be no more voices.

The last psychologist Craig saw told me to use tough love on him.That was his answer to Craig's problems. He also told Craig that he was not capable of holding a job and that he needed to learn to socialize in a special class, this for a young man who had always been so popular. I was willing to take care of him if I had to for the rest of his and my life. It was the attitude I took. Assuming Craig would live to 80, I would will myself to live to 110. I would work and take care of him.

At the funeral I didn't want everything to be so morbid. I had lots of balloons, we played Rocky Mountain High because he went to school in Colorado and one friend sang a song he wrote.

Also, after the funeral I had to deal with that last psychologist and see him. I needed to talk to him and tell him he took away the last shred of Craig's integrity by laughing at him when he said Craig couldn't hold a job. He shuffled the papers around on his desk like he did when Craig was there. I sat in front of him and said, "Look me in the face and see my pain and feel my anger. Just because a child may be mentally ill doesn't mean they aren't sensitive and don't have feelings." If anything, their sensitivity is heightened then. After 20 minutes he escorted me to the door. He never apologized. I, on the other hand, had said my piece.

I'm all for people going to support groups, but, personally, The Compassionate Friends group didn't work for me. I felt like people there were competing. "I lost one child," says one. "I lost two children," says another. "I lost three children," says a third. It was like a contest about who suffered the most. At suicide survivors groups, participants would compete over whose death was the bloodiest. I became my own support system. I told friends I wanted to talk about Craig and my friends were very supportive and stayed close.

My daughter Lois was very close to Craig. I realized much later that not enough attention is paid to siblings. Lois put her grief aside to help me those first five years. She never had the opportunity to complete her grief because of her concern for me. When she realized I would survive, she was able to grieve.

In those first years I would go to bed at night and say to God, "If you want me, I'm yours." Every morning I'd wake up and say, "Well, I guess you still want me here." It was the fifth anniversary of Craig's death, as I stood at his grave that I accepted the fact that I wasn't going to die from my grief. Standing there I also knew I needed to do something with my life. I had to find a way to get beyond grief and accept the fact that I needed to create a life for myself.

For 15 years I had a temporary personnel business, five branches of them throughout Pennsylvania. On the third year after Craig's death I sold the business and decided to take a year off. After that I realized I didn't have the energy or drive to start another business. I got my real estate license and knew immediately that wasn't what I wanted either. I went to Guatemala to visit a friend for a month and fell in love with the place, staying for three years.

Something magical happened during that time. Guatemala was slow paced, nurturing. There were no telephones, no cars, no pressures. The only thing you had to focus on was how you were feeling. It was very spiritual. I learned to paint and liked it very much. I ended up doing a cookbook in Spanish and English from a wonderful array of restaurants in the area. I would go into the restaurant and ask them for their recipes. I got a photographer to take photos and ended up publishing it myself. The money I made from that I used to start a children's library in Antigua.

I was still feeling tremendous guilt. I should have been able to keep my son alive. It was my greatest purpose on earth, and I failed. While in Guatemala I realized the doctors couldn't even keep him alive. I was told even if he'd been strapped down, he would have found a way to end his life if he wasn't meant to live. I needed to let go of the burden I put on myself and do something. Eventually, I realized that I had good qualities; I have capabilities; I'm salvageable; maybe I can contribute something to this world.

But then Guatemala started to get dangerous, particularly for Americans. I still wasn't ready to go back to the states, with all its pressures. So I headed to Mexico for one year where I started a soup kitchen for homeless women. The needs there were so great. I went there to focus on myself, but saw how others lived and knew I had to help them. My life was good in comparison to theirs, and I knew I should be grateful.

I came back to Scottsdale because my daughter got engaged, but still didn't have energy to go back to work. I had been on my own too long being able to do what I wanted when I wanted. So I decided to do volunteer work for the Mental Health Association of Arizona in public speaking and education. They have a program called "Options" where they go into the high schools and educate teachers and students on the symptoms of depression to avoid suicide. The next day I went to one school to observe, and the director asked if I wanted to speak. I excused myself to the bathroom and while in there told God that I didn't know what to say. "Tell you what, I said. I'll open my mouth, and you provide the words." I went on stage, opened my mouth and haven't stopped since.

I worked as a volunteer for a year. Then I was asked to actually work for them with pay. I told them I needed to work from my home, have no more than a 20 hour week and make my own schedule. They agreed. I'm now a consultant on a contract basis.

What I do is go into districts and meet with principals, telling them about the program. The principals decide which schools want the program. I meet with school psychologists and then conduct the program in an assembly for the teachers. Some districts have all staff members including bus drivers, cafeteria help and assistants attend. They are educated first. With kids, I go into individual classes, keeping it small so they can ask questions. When I tell my story, I bring pictures to pass around so kids get to know my son. I tell them about Craig and his popularity at school, how active in sports he was, how he killed himself and the symptoms to look for.

One time I got Craig's picture back, and it had lots of fingerprints on it. How great, I thought, that Craig had touched all these people. It reminded me of a dream where I thought I saw Craig on the street. Craig let me and everyone know that Heaven is what you want it to be. "It isn't the same for everyone," he said, "because that wouldn't make everyone happy. I'm helping boys in distress. I'm taking someone up to heaven." And off he went. I felt like Craig was reaching these boys before they were in distress. It was such a connection. The dream had gone full circle. It was telling me what Craig was doing, and I didn't realize at the time it would be something I would be doing too.

Kids from the classrooms have written letters to me and said they have considered suicide. Many say if they did kill themselves, their family wouldn't be affected by it. They see how I'm affected, and it makes them rethink the fact that their families would, indeed, miss them. I find it so sad to go to school and see how many kids know someone who has committed suicide. At least 75 percent of most classes raise their hand when I ask. Many of these same kids are affected by depression too. So few go for help.

I love what I do. I love meeting educators. I also speak at Mental Health conferences and do public service announcements.

Kids ask if I'm doing this to prevent suicides. I tell them I'm doing it so I won't be part of the shame attached to mental illness. Part of what drives me is three years after Craig died, a cousin committed suicide. I found out he had the same symptoms as Craig for the 10 years before he died. But it was kept quiet because of the shame and stigma attached to mental illness. I remember the doctors asked me when I first brought Craig in to see them, if any of my family had mental illness. I said "no" at the time. If I had known and been able to give that information to the doctors, perhaps they would have been able to come up with a more accurate diagnosis and proper treatment, which might have saved Craig's life. That's why I won't be part of the shame and stigma.

Craig had lots of stuffed animals he loved. On my bed sits his favorite teddy bear. When I look at it, I think of Craig as I do when I light candles and bring special purple flowers to a church in my travels and to his grave when we visit in Pennsylvania. Purple is a healing color and that is what I try to do every day now. Although I haven't yet discovered the answer, I know there was a purpose to Craig's life and that not everybody's purpose takes a full lifetime to achieve.

Observations of Nancy

Teenage suicide is escalating at an alarming rate. Suicide is the third leading cause of death for 15-25 year olds.

Unfortunately, suicide is little understood by most people. A person could inherit a gene for a pre-disposition to a mental illness. If you are a relative of the person who died, people may conclude there is also something wrong with you. Nancy has found that sometimes parents can be ignored by others, although in her case, she always felt people to be very empathetic towards her. To avoid problems with others, some parents will hide from the truth of their child's problems and 'live a lie' as Nancy says her relative did. Nancy talks about mental illness to show people they are just contributing to the shame and stigma attached to mental illness by keeping silent. She is doing her work to bring attention to mental illness...that it does exist...but at the same time, it is responsive to treatment if a proper diagnosis can be made, and the freedom to talk about it is there.

Nancy admits that although she was a good mother, for a long time she had trouble coping with the guilt of not being able to save her son. Two other thoughts and reactions parents have that affect their efforts to heal from the death include: (1) a personal abandonment by the child that he preferred to die rather than be alive with you and (2) fearing for other family members. For Nancy, only through lots of nurturing was she able to find peace within and new meaning in all that has happened.

I can't help but think of Nancy as I recall the old Serenity Prayer by Reinhold Niebuhr: "God give us grace to accept with serenity the things that cannot be changed, courage to change the things which should be changed and the wisdom to distinguish the one from the other." Craig could no longer deal with his mental anguish and felt so hopeless and helpless after that last doctor took away his last shred of dignity, he wanted to end the pain. Nancy knows she could not have saved her son and found a way to accept that. Now her goal is 'to change the things she can' by making a difference in the area of bringing attention to mental illness.

8

Justin

> *"For three years I couldn't function after the death of my son…It was not our first encounter with losing a child…I had three miscarriages…"*
>
> Bonnie

For three years I could not function. The sudden death of my 18-year-old son was the cause. My husband, Don, was just as devastated but after two weeks was able to go back to work. It was more than three years before I could lift myself out of my depression and constant tears and force myself to leave the house for more than just shopping for food.

Justin was a junior in high school in 1992. A quiet boy, he found a niche in writing for the school newspaper and enjoyed interviewing people for the stories he wrote. This surprised us because he had always been somewhat shy.

Justin was always a good child. We were proud of him. He was always thoughtful to others, very caring.

I remember one time when he brought a friend home who was rather seedy looking. I questioned him as to why he had befriended this boy. "He's having trouble, mom," was the answer, "and I thought I could help him out." Again, proud of his ways, there was nothing more to be said.

One night he went out for a coke with another friend and the friend's girlfriend. I didn't question when he'd be home because I trusted him. They ended up spending the night at the boy's aunt's house. I did not know the aunt was away for the weekend. At 6 a.m. we got a call from the police to come to the hospital. When we arrived we found out Justin was dead. He had been drinking vodka, fell asleep on the couch as the couple went into the bedroom and aspirated (throwing up and swallowing it again). A half empty bottle was found next to him. After the autopsy we were told the alcohol level was 4.0. Justin had never had a drink before in his life.

We discovered later that not only was alcohol the leading cause of death in teens, but it was also the cause of many deaths of first time drinkers whose bodies could not handle the liquor. To complicate matters Justin had asthma.

Needless to say we were shocked and devastated. We could not even drive home. Family members picked us up, but our other children, two sons, were out of the country and our daughter without a phone. By nighttime we were all together.

Being around the family for two weeks helped us a lot. I was so glad they were there for us. I was also scared to think what would happen when they left. They were our support. But we knew that eventually they would all have to leave, and we would be alone with only our memories. Everywhere I looked in the house Justin was there. I wanted to move, just to get away from it all. Don agreed, but it never came about. Now we are okay with it.

We both cried a lot. We still do at times. There was a numbness about the whole thing, an unreality that hung in the air. I found I couldn't function. I couldn't do everyday things. I couldn't even get up, I was so filled with grief. I wouldn't talk to my friends. But I think they understood and left me alone. They were there for me three years later, and I am thankful for that.

Don and I talked and helped each other get through it together. I know there are many people who grow apart when something like this happens, but not us. Don is stronger than I am, but that doesn't lessen his grief. We are both open about our feelings to each other and our friends.

Surprisingly, there was no anger. Our son was old enough to know better. He was very aware of what could happen. He was taking a drivers ed course at school that very semester. What I will always question and can't understand is why he did it?

Eventually, I realized I was only thinking of death, not of the life he lived. It was time to think of the good memories, not the loss. It was time to think of what he meant to us, what he had accomplished in his short life and his innate goodness. I also found I needed to go back to work, to be with people. It was time to move on. It was almost three years by then.

I discovered months later work had been the best thing for me. With an active mind, I would not dwell on Justin's death 24 hours a day. The worst thing I did during those years was pull away from everyone and everything. It gave me too much time to think, and sometimes that can be dangerous to your well being.

Knowing what I know now, a Christian counselor could have helped me put it in a better perspective and deal with the death a lot sooner. But I definitely know that neither books nor grieving groups were for me.

This was not our first encounter with losing a child. I had three miscarriages in-between my four living children. Each time it happened we cried and prayed. It affects you, but I know it was not meant to be and that is what comforts me. It is also not the same as losing a grown child who you have nurtured and watched grow up.

Holidays are hard. On Justin's birthday, July 2, we talk about him a lot. Last year we were in the mountains with family members and cousins and on his birthday the cousins and others wrote cards wishing Justin a happy birthday and taped them up. It is comforting to know he is not forgotten by others.

Observations of Bonnie

Bonnie agrees that she has a long way to go. The interview was very difficult for her. The memories were overpowering and at times she had to wipe her eyes and pause as she caught her breath. It is certainly nothing to be ashamed of. Most of us will do this for the rest of our lives. We loved our children more than anything. Our heart tells us they are gone even though our minds consider it impossible and incomprehensible that a child could die before a parent. It is not the order of how life was meant to be. Sadly though, it is reality.

Don could talk about his son with a smile on his face, obviously remembering the good times. His strength helped Bonnie deal with her own demons. The rest she worked out herself. For months or even years one can feel lost, but through personal efforts and the passage of time, healing begins to take place. And so it was with Bonnie.

There are others, though, who find it more difficult and their lives just stop. If your grief goes to this extreme, it is advisable to seek professional help. This does not mean you are crazy, but just that you need help getting back on track. Therapy can give the reassurance needed to get on with your life.

When the interview ended, Bonnie breathed a sigh of relief that she had made it through intact. It was an accomplishment for her and much to her surprise her face had a look on it that said, "That wasn't as bad as I thought it would be," and her lips curled into a slight smile. Everyday we take a small step. That is the way it will always be and accepting that, we move on as Bonnie does each day, holding close to her heart the memory of her son.

9

Jimmy

"My work with The Compassionate Friends has always been a tribute not only to my son who died but also to my surviving children. Somewhere along the line you make the decision, 'Am I going to be bitter or better?' It seems like his life was so short that it was up to me to do something for him..."

Diana

After 23 years, you would think that I have dealt with everything possible in regards to the death of my 10-year-old son, Jimmy. It is always startling to me when I'm caught off guard. When I hear a song he liked or see a piece of clothing similar to what he used to wear, I think of him. I feel tears well up, but instead of being upset, I like it! One of the biggest fears we have is that we'll forget, but we never do. Somewhere along the line I decided to concentrate on the joy the events of his life brought me rather than on the events of the day he died, and that made the day and everything easier to deal with.

Jimmy died accidentally from a gunshot wound to the head in 1977. Jimmy, his stepdad and my brother went out into the desert target shooting near our Arizona home so I could get ready for a New Year's

Eve party we were having. Something went terribly wrong. My brother picked up one of the guns, and it went off accidentally. Life changed forever after that moment.

I heard sirens near the house and remember thinking, "I'm so glad we were having a party in our home where mostly neighbors could walk over and not have to deal with the crazzies on the streets New Year's Eve. My family would be home and intact." What I really heard was the ambulance carrying my son to the hospital.

I got a call to go to the emergency center. Jimmy had been in an accident, I was told. I thought maybe he had fallen down and gotten a bump on his head or injured an ankle. I had convinced myself of it. I heard what I wanted to hear. Finally, my husband got through to me what had happened. But I was a master at denial. Jimmy, my beautiful son, everything you could ever want in a child…no one would shoot Jimmy…a mistake had been made. I stayed calm; I was not stressed at all because I had made up my mind everything was okay.

When the doctor came into the waiting room, he said very coldly, "Had he lived he would have been a vegetable." He turned around and walked out. What was he saying? I was horribly confused. Whole segments of time were lost then. I remember very little of what happened at the hospital except for that one question, "Where do you want the body sent?" The mind can block out what it doesn't want to hear. Were they talking about my Jimmy, calling him a body? I was astounded.

I did know that I had two daughters at home, 7 and 11, and I had to get home. People were coming to the house. I called a neighbor for the name of a mortuary and she, in turn called everyone and told them what had happened. The neighbor told me months later that I appeared very cool, calm, so matter of fact. Deep shock had consumed me.

In-between jobs, I was supposed to start a new one on the day of the funeral. For several months after that day I didn't work. I muddled through each day. Even though my husband was Jimmy's stepfather, his pain and grief were every bit as intense as mine. I never doubted that for a minute. When someone would say to him, "Well, it was only your stepchild," I thought he would rip their eyebrows out.

In 1977 there were no self-help books, no grief-bereavement organizations, no talk shows, nothing. You didn't talk about death and grieving. During this time I was very afraid that I was put on earth for things to be snatched away from me. I became overprotective and probably made my two girls nuts.

It wasn't until eight months later that I heard about a brand new organization, The Compassionate Friends (TCF) on the Phil Donahue talk show. There was no chapter where I lived and so three months later I became a founding member of Phoenix's first chapter. I had been feeling isolated, not knowing many people and having no family other than my husband and daughters. This monthly group was a blessing. I finally had people understand what I was feeling.

Two years later I moved to California where I lived until 1997. I was divorced (and still single) and thought that I was doing okay. Around the house were photos of all the kids. When my new friends came over, they would ask about the pictures. "Who is this one?" they would say pointing to Jimmy. I realized as I stumbled through this that I still needed to be with other people that had lost a child. I started a chapter in Riverside in 1981. Little did I realize that what I learned from the people who came was far more healing to me than what I could do for them. Every time you reach out to someone you're healing yourself.

Never in my wildest dreams did I ever imagine I would become the national executive director of this organization. The organization grew tremendously through the '80's, and I served in every capacity: as newsletter editor, as regional coordinator, on the board of directors and chairman of the national conference in 1996. The plan was to retire from the organization after the conference, but because of changes occurring on the national level, I was asked to serve as interim director until one could be found. I realized I believed completely in this organization. It is a lifeline for thousands of families throughout the country and around the world. Except for my immediate family, the most important people in my life were part of this organization, a special type of family for me. At the last moment I submitted a resume and was offered the job of executive director, a position I held until fall of 2000. I packed everything and moved to Illinois, TCF headquarters.

My work with The Compassionate Friends has always been a tribute not only to Jimmy but also to my surviving children. Somewhere along the line you make the decision, "Am I going to be bitter or better?" It seems like his life was so short that it was up to me to do something for him. He was a neat little boy. He was convinced he would be a professional baseball player and off season, a cowboy. When I'm doing things for the organization, it is my "Jimmy time."

It was very hard to leave my son buried in Arizona and move. Intellectually, I knew he wasn't there, but I felt like I was abandoning my child. Every place I move I make a "Jimmy garden." I put in his favorite color flowers in the dirt or in potted plants. I have a rock he picked up in the desert that he liked, and it is always with me for placement in the gardens.

Holidays, particularly Thanksgiving, are always difficult. He was born November 16, and I brought him home Thanksgiving. I have a funny looking turkey made out of pine cones and pipe cleaners Jimmy made one year for me. Each year, it is always part of the centerpiece on my table.

He also gave me a candle holder one Christmas made out of chunks of wood. "Will you think of me when you use them?" Jimmy asked me. My answer to him was "Why in the world would I have to use candle holders to think of you because you're always here." One week later he was no longer there. On significant days such as his birthday, Christmas, Thanksgiving and New Year's, the candle holders are always in a prominent place in my home even with the crystal candle holders and the fancy silver plates. Sometimes I just take them out and light them if I feel a need to be connected.

I'm sorry there is a need for TCF, yet I'm so glad they're here. I remember how alone and isolated I was, thinking I was the only one that had ever gone through this. Seeing the changes that have taken place towards grieving families and knowing TCF and all support groups have been instrumental in changing the public attitude towards grieving is very rewarding. Society didn't know how to deal with it. You expect to bury your parents and there is even a chance of burying your spouse, as I had to do at age 21, but you never expect to bury your child. I know everyone says that but because it's so true, it bears repeating.

People used to say to me, "I always wanted to mention your child, but I was afraid it would remind you" (as though we're ever going to forget). TCF encourages people to talk about their children. "Yes," I tell them, "you'll see us cry, but mention that child's name because parents love to hear someone else talk about their child. People call and ask me if TCF has something written to tell others how to deal with a friend's child's death. They have the resources, and these friends get help earlier, in turn helping the parent to deal with it earlier too. Parents and families are seen now days after a death.

Those who have worked through the grief process and no longer attend meetings, still want to be on the mailing list or subscribe to the national magazine. They want that connection. It is my hope that many will choose to stay connected to be the next hand to reach out.

It is important for people to understand this is an ongoing process and that little pieces of grief will be with you for the rest of your life. One of the things happening now is that Jimmy's friends are at an age when they are marrying and having children. I wonder what his children would have been like. When my daughters were married, it was a happy affair, but an element of sadness tore at my heart because he wasn't there to enjoy this with us. The same was true when my two grandchildren were born.

I have learned a lot of lessons as the direct result of my son's death. One is that I see how Jimmy's death affected my daughters. How they bring up their children, for example, is clearly the result of some of the things they experienced because of their brother's death. The major changes that have happened in my life are because of the gifts Jimmy gave me from his life and his death.

I never thought I could say there is joy in my life again, but there is. I never thought I would be content with life. I really believed those first few years after his death I was going to plod along forever, and it was never going to be good again. But I like my life. I can't imagine doing anything else right now. There is only one reason I would come to this organization. I'm not saying I'm glad my child is dead. It took me a long time to learn the lesson that I had no control over what happened that day and as a parent we think we have control over what happens to our children. But because that day happened, here's where I am now. Yes, I miss him and I love him and there is not a day that goes by that I don't ask myself, "What if…" There's nothing I can do about that. Instead, I can continue doing what I'm doing in his honor, in his memory and continue to like my life and the person I've become.

Observations of Diana

For many years The Compassionate Friends was Diana's lifeline. The work she continues to do is 'Jimmy time.' Every time she reaches out to someone who is in pain, she is doing that because of Jimmy. Jimmy is no longer here, but the time she would have devoted to him is now devoted to helping others.

And Diana believes completely and follows the slogan of the TCF organization: **We Need Not Walk Alone.** *She tries to be there for those who need her, and she tries to educate those who care about bereaved families. She knows that only through education can others know what to say, how to act and how to give the emotional support needed during the journey through grief. She also realizes how important it is for parents to have an outlet to talk freely about their child and their grief. TCF is also helpful to grandparents, siblings and other adult family members.*

She emphasized throughout our conversation that if you become involved with an organization you don't have to become everyone's best friend. Grief is very personal and unique, and how we respond and react to it is due to other circumstances in our lives. Some people will be negative all their lives and just because their child dies doesn't mean that they're going to change. Others will find new meaning to their life as Diana did. It was a hard lesson for her to learn but an important one.

Diana also says that there is no guarantee that this loss will be as bad as it gets. Other things may happen that will be hurtful also. That's part of life. You learn how to respond differently and know you can survive no matter what you're going through. She sees how far she has come in her life and is pleased with the results.

10

Dusty and Afton

"After both our children died we thought of having more...but instead decided to adopt and help a child from another country, giving him a loving home he wouldn't have been able to have..."

Joe and Wanda

On a gravel road in the countryside of Iowa, August of 1992, a 17-year-old boy crashed into the passenger side of an automobile carrying my two children and my mother. The teen was not on drugs, nor had he had any alcohol to drink. No speed limits were posted in the area. My mom and our two children died on impact. He was let off. There was nothing we or the prosecutors could do. My two children Dusty, 9, and Afton, 7, were dead. So was my mother...Wanda

It was like we were in a dream. Wanda and I didn't want to believe it. I was mad at God. I prayed a lot. I knew the kids wouldn't want us to feel this way. They'd want us to go on with our lives and be happy. It was a struggle at first...Joe

I was so mad at the kid that drove the car and that no charges were filed. Then my minister said something to me that made a lot of sense. "You don't know what this teen is feeling inside. Don't forget, he has to live with this, too, for the rest of his life." To keep going, I kept busy. At night when I couldn't sleep, I would bake just to keep from lying there and thinking. I got very depressed to the point where Joe was worried, and eventually, I got professional help. I wish now I would have gone sooner for help. It's like anything else; if I was an alcoholic, until I faced up to it, I would never get better. Joe was my rock and stuck by me through all the bad times instead of throwing in the towel. We had a good marriage before the kids died, but our marriage became stronger afterwards…Wanda

Our children, Dusty and Afton were both very shy, like Joe. Dusty was on the baseball team, and they both sang in the church choir. Afton, a very soft-hearted child, liked to dress up and wear jewelry. She was a good little shopper. Both liked to fish, Afton more so. I don't enjoy shopping as much now. It's not fun and too painful, and Joe has not gone fishing since then either. As siblings, they got along beautifully. They didn't fight like the typical brother and sister. They were just very close. When they died together, Joe and I said, "Why did God take both of them?" They were so close in life on earth, maybe it was meant for them to die together and be together forever…Wanda

If it wasn't for our faith or church, Joe and I couldn't have gotten through this. I learned after Afton died, from a mother of a little girl in her kidnastic class, that Afton said, "I'm not afraid to die. I know I'll go to heaven to be with Jesus." We knew they had a strong faith, and we had brought them up right by taking them to church and Sunday school. We don't want to sound over-religious, but we know with God's strength, we've gotten through this. Even though at first we were angry at God for doing this to us, we know now He has carried us through these years and helped us…Wanda

Wanda and I found many people treated us as though we had changed completely after our children died. One friend said to me less than a week after the funeral, "Do you realize out of all the couples that have children die, 60-80 percent divorce." What a cold statement for someone to say to us! And the statistic is not even accurate. It is much less than that. Other friends said they would come by and take care of us, that we'd get tired of them being around all the time. But they didn't come around. They said we'd changed; we weren't the same Joe and Wanda they had known before. Did they really think you could have both your children die and not change? Inside we were still the same friends to them, on the outside, sure we were different. Who wouldn't be after such a tragedy!…Joe

When the people stayed away, Joe and I got a whole new group of friends from a card club we started, church and fellow workers. We began calling these people to do things with us, and we have become close. Looking back, I guess the others just didn't understand and didn't know how to handle it at the time. We don't get uptight about the little things anymore. Nothing can compare to such a devastating tragedy…Wanda

After our children died Joe and I thought of having more, naturally. We could have. But instead, we decided to adopt and help a child from another country, giving him a loving home he wouldn't otherwise have a chance to have. Two and a half years later we adopted a four month old Korean boy from Seoul and named him Hunter. The process took nine months. We chose this road knowing that when a mother in Korea has a child out of wedlock, they are shunned and the child would be too. Our social worker wanted us to get another soon after, but we said no. We now live our lives for Hunter, but we still need to do things in memory of Dusty and Afton…Wanda

Many memorials have been set up to keep their memory alive for us. Joe and I have adopted two miles of highway in Iowa. A sign indicates it is in the children's memory. It is cleaned twice a year. Family and friends have helped over the years, but recently I prefer doing it alone. It gives me time to think and be alone…Wanda

Wanda and I gave three pictures to our church in memory of Dusty and Afton and a plaque on each picture indicates that it comes from us.

We have bought the fair queen trophy for our local fair in memory of the children. We did a special remembrance for the high school's senior class in the years they would have graduated. The school yearbooks were dedicated to each of them during what would have been their senior year. For the confirmation class at church we gave each student a gold plaque with a confirmation verse on it in Dusty and Afton's memory. For the children's birthdays and the anniversary of their death we put flowers in our church, and it is recognized in the church bulletin. Their graves are decorated for holidays such as Christmas with a small tree, and donations are given to the support groups Alive Alone and The Compassionate Friends who were so helpful to us…Joe

But the greatest memorial is in the Precious Moments Chapel in Missouri, where a mural of Dusty and Afton playing catch with a baseball, along with other children who have died, was painted by a friend, Sam Butcher, who built the church after his own son died. It is a huge mural in the front part of the church, and every 20 minutes tours go through, and a guide tells either our children's story or one of the other children depicted on the mural. Joe and I feel it is one of the greatest living memorials we could give to them…Wanda

We believe the best thing is to talk about our children and not to let their memory die. Joe and I firmly believe we will continue to do these things and hope, in the process, we can also be of help to others going through the death of a child…Wanda

Hunter knows about Dusty and Afton. Wanda and I talk about them all the time. Pictures are all over. One night Hunter broke down crying his heart out. "What's the matter?" I asked. "I want to see my brother and sister in person," Hunter said. He was beside himself. It was hard to explain and hard on me. I said, "Only when you go to heaven will you see them." Hunter's answer was, "I want to die then." "No," I said, "You're too young. You don't want to die yet. We want to see them too, but we can't." Hunter woke up crying a couple of nights because of bad dreams. "Go to sleep and have sweet dreams," we told him. "Sweet dreams are about Dusty and Afton and grandma and good things like that." Since then he hasn't had nightmares...Joe

We want Hunter to know he's adopted and about his brother and sister dying. Joe and I want to be open about both of these issues so he feels he can talk to us about them at any time. He goes to the cemetery with us, likes to put flowers on the stones and kiss the picture. It's hard for such a young child...Wanda

If we know of a child in the area we live who has died, Joe and I go over and try to help the parents as much as possible. It is what we want and what Dusty and Afton would want us to do. We try to tell these parents that it is important to understand husbands and wives grieve differently and to accept those differences within each other. What helped us most was having a strong faith, having each other, being patient with each other, going to support groups, doing memorials and talking to each other about the child. The more we talk about our children, the more it seems to help...Wanda

I tell parents: you'll think it'll never get better, but it does. Time does help heal. You always have a hole in your heart, but you learn to live with the pain. You're still going to cry. Joe and I do to this day, but we know that this is the hand that God dealt us, and we have to live with it...Wanda

Observations of Joe and Wanda

Losing two children at the same time—you think it can't happen, but it does and to many. It took strength, courage and the ability to see that although God dealt a cruel blow, we must accept what has happened if we are to survive. So it was with Joe and Wanda. They could have been bitter and angry at a judicial system that has no punishment for drivers who kill innocent children and adults. They could have found God to be cruel and uncaring. But they realized no good comes from anger and hate.

So they turned their energies towards hope, healing and comforting others. One of the organizations that was a great help to them, Alive Alone, is

for bereaved parents, whose only child or all children are deceased. They provided for Joe and Wanda a self-help network of people to contact and a publication to promote communication and healing. They were able to look to a more positive future through this organization and through The Compassionate Friends, who have very similar goals.

Together they have moved on with their lives by leaving memorials to honor their children and by adopting a child and giving him every ounce of love left in them. There are a lot of children in the world that can be helped and many adoption agency newsletters are begging people to adopt and give these children from foreign lands a loving home in which to be raised. Joe and Wanda know they did what was right for them and say even though Hunter is a handful (and what little boy isn't), he is being brought up to understand, love and respect the memory of Dusty and Afton.

Joe and Wanda's faith, church, support groups and knowing their children would want them to be happy have made their journey a little easier.

11

Jay

> *"The only way to continue our child's legacy in a great way is to think positively...it takes a long time before you can...however, when you do, your child will lead you...and help you define your life."*
>
> Kathy

I do believe in God and the hereafter and this has helped me survive the loss of my 16-year-old son, Jay. At first nothing helped. I was in deep shock and completely inconsolable. Here was a beautiful young boy with so much promise. The pain was unbearable. When I came out of it many months later, it was like my body was frozen and I was thawing out. My husband and I even had chest pains, like we were having a heart attack. It was the grief, total grief, we were experiencing, nothing more. What helps me now are friends, the bereavement groups joined, the work I do to help other parents survive and what I accomplish in honor of my son.

In 1992 16-year-old Jay, the second of my four children, was a senior in high school. He was a very mature boy for his age; he always seemed older. He was a year ahead of other kids his age academically and so acted older. As I think back, it was a mistake how it played out in the social aspect of starting him in school early. It would have been better for him to be with kids his own age and not be a year younger, even though he was academically ahead.

Jay was lively, spirited, brave, intelligent, caring and someone who was his own person. One of my favorite memories of Jay was when he was in third grade. He decided to change his name. I named this child, Jamie, but when he discovered a girl in his class with the same name, he decided to tell the teacher his name was changed to Jay. This child definitely had a mind of his own, but I liked the name Jay, so we let him make this change. As a teenager Jay loved the guitar, girls, sports and fishing, along with being very business-minded. His senior year he was working on a scholarship for marketing, using our family business as his thesis. Sadly, my reality now is that there is a scholarship in his name from the marketing class at the high school.

One weekend he wanted to see a friend who attended college in Lansing, Michigan. We lived in Temperance, a few hours away. I didn't want him to go. The car he drove was not in very good condition, and he had not been driving that long. We even considered driving him there or making him take a bus. We told him, "If you can find a good car, you can go." He found a boy with a sports car who ended up driving very fast, very dangerously…a real thrill seeker. We later found out Jay pleaded with the driver to slow down, but we figured the boy was probably trying to show off for Jay, since Jay was very popular in school. We got the call every parent dreads in the middle of the night. The car had gone out of control and crashed. Of the three in the car, he was the only one to die.

When we first lost Jay, one of the items we received was a poem from a friend of his, a girl whose message in the poem was "love me, but let me go on to the next world, and every time you think of me, go out and do something good for someone else." At first this meant nothing, was almost an irritating thought, but as time moved on, I looked for an answer, a way to survive. I got lucky. A friend I worked with was president of the Parent Teacher Association (PTA) at Jay's school and got me involved in the group. She needed someone to take over work with legislation in her group. At the time the graduated licensing was an issue in Michigan, and I seemed the logical choice. This was right up my alley. The bill changed the way kids got drivers licenses. They needed to learn all the rules, practice driving more and only then qualify to get full driving privileges.The law also made parents more responsible. I ended up testifying before the Senate for the bill, and recruited more than 150 postcards from parents in the area. The bill passed, and I found that it gave me a great sense of relief that I could do something good in Jay's honor. This was when I remembered the poem, and I have continued these efforts in PTA legislative work with any type of legislation that comes across the state affecting children. For example, there are playground safety issues, driving laws, underage drinking, tobacco laws, pornography on the internet, violence laws and drug laws.

At the high school I also helped getting speakers for S.A.D.D.'s mock drunk driving accident program. At a reenactment, kids are shown first hand what really can happen during and after a car accident. It is very graphic but brings the point home. I still continue to help on this important issue even though all of my kids have graduated from the high school. It is my personal way to survive all this. I do not tell people that. I just do it. For me.

My bereavement groups have also been my savior. There's nothing like sharing with people who really know your pain. I've made some close friends in my group and their help cannot even be described. I believe anyone who has lost a child should join a bereavement group that deals with the loss of children specifically. There is much common ground they can share. It has taught me many lessons, such as not everyone grieves the same. My husband grieves much differently than I, but that doesn't mean he doesn't care. Even one of my sons went to some meetings when siblings were invited and spoke to the group. He found it very healing. No one else in my family has gone to any of their meetings.

In our town there is a new bereavement group called FOCUS (Families of Children United in Spirit) which is for all bereaved people, not just parents. Grandparents, aunts, uncles and step-parents can come too. Once a month we help other people by being there for them. We find these people, or they are referred to us. In our meetings we are able to say to them, "Hey, I was there once, too." It is a great support system.

One thing I always remember is a relative one year responding to my comment of, "I am really having a tough Christmas." With all honesty, she said, "Really, and why is that?" She didn't get it. In our FOCUS group, everyone gets it!

My husband found it very difficult to talk about Jay at first, but now he can share a memory once in a while. While my bereavement group comforts me, he does not feel comfortable sharing his feelings. The group helped me to know that everyone grieves differently. My husband deals with his grief privately, although when in church, I always notice a few misty tears in his eyes.

I have a table in the hall with a candle on it, and on holidays or if I feel it's important to light the candle on special occasions, I do it. I don't get anyone's permission. I'm hoping as the years go on it will be okay to say, "Let's talk about something silly Jay did" or "Help me light the candle." We do not have an open family forum about this topic, but I would like to change that.

The best advice I can offer to bereaved parents or family members is to hang in there. At first nothing helps, as the pain is really unbearable. How can anyone make sense of losing a child? It's not supposed to happen. Our children are to bury us, we are not supposed to bury them. Try to take care of your physical health; eat and sleep right when possible. After some time, no magic number, you will begin to feel somewhat comfortable. I believe we are never the same, but our new self begins to get comfortable. Try different things to help yourself. Join a bereavement group, share ideas they have for you, volunteer in your community and accept everyone's way of dealing with grief.

There are only two ways to think, positively or negatively, and the only way to continue our child's legacy in a great way is to think positively. This is easier said than done, and I believe it takes a long time before you can begin to think positively. However, when you do, your child will lead you. I believe Jay leads me and helps me define my life in a more positive way. He will always be alive in my heart and in the hearts of those who loved him.

Observations of Kathy

Kathy is a unique individual who has found her place in helping others through their grief. This is one of the most treasured gifts one person can give another. Be there to talk, to listen and to just be silent. Words aren't always necessary. A touch from another person, a hug or even a silent prayer can show others how much they are cared about and most of all, an understanding of how much they are hurting. It is this kind of thoughtfulness and support that helps others put their lives back together.

Unfortunately, she has yet to get her entire family (husband and three children) to deal with Jay's death in a way that is comfortable for all of them to share. She knows they all loved Jay, think about him all the time and will never forget what happened. But she would love for all of them to celebrate special occasions together, to have special remembrances. However, she realizes it is important to let each of the family members use their own methods of coping. This is far better than becoming frustrated and unhappy in a marriage and life in general. She is aware through her grief group FOCUS that everyone grieves differently, and it is not for her to say how her family should grieve and deal with Jay's death. However family members find peace and solace, we must respect that.

She also believes that Jay is up there looking after all of them and leading her forward to do the work she was meant to do. God brought the PTA and FOCUS into her life, knowing she needed help and support, and she is thankful He and Jay are both watching over her.

12

Susan

> *"My personality told me I could handle everything myself...and not rely on other people...It was not that I didn't appreciate the offers, but I just didn't accept them. I accepted my fate as something I had to live with..."*
>
> Maryanne

It is hard for any parent to bury a child, but when you are in your seventies and your 43-year-old daughter goes to sleep at night and never wakes up, you question why God did this to her and to me so soon after my husband died.

Susan died of acute asthma very suddenly in January 1992. She'd had a few bouts with asthma when younger, but it was never that serious. During her childhood she was active in sports, dancing, singing and music. When she was 21-years-old, a car accident crushed her larynx, affecting her voice for the rest of her life. She talked just above a whisper the rest of her life but adjusted to it. You never heard her complain about what she was dealt. Her courage never stopped her from doing anything in her life. She had a great character; undeniably, one of the best I've ever seen, even though she was my own.

Susan was president of her state area sorority group. When she got up to speak, you could hear a pin drop. Even with her voice so soft and breathy, everybody stopped and listened to what she had to say. Because of the accident she sometimes had trouble breathing during this time. Doctors said she had sleep apnea also.

I needed toe surgery that January so Susan offered to take me to the doctor the next day. She came to my house the night before, said she wasn't feeling very well and went to sleep early. The next morning I went into the bedroom to get her up so she could take me, and I couldn't wake her. Her body felt cold. I attributed the coldness to the ceiling fan and called 911. They were very close by, but gave me instructions for CPR. It didn't do any good. She had died hours before.

My husband had died the previous year from cancer and now Susan. They were both buried very close to my home. At first I went often because I would always pass the cemetery when I left the house and felt guilty if I didn't stop. Now I go to leave flowers and take care of the markers every so often, but the guilt is gone. I have not done any memorials in her honor, nor do I do anything special on holidays or birthdays.

Susan was always a delightful person inside and out. She was very sensitive to other's needs, outgoing, considerate and always had a smile when she walked through a door. She had been divorced eight years at the time of her death and had worked as an executive administrative assistant to Hollywood Race Track. It was a prime position. Her duties allowed her to deal with many celebrities which she found extremely fascinating.

Recently, I found myself going through some papers of hers that I had saved and came across a letter she had written to my mother, her grandmother. My mom was going to have hip surgery the next day and Susan told my mom that when her car accident had happened, her faith and courage kept her going and that she knew her grandmother would do the same. Here was a 24-year-old talking to a 65 year-old woman, her maturity clearly showing.

My religious beliefs helped me and strengthened my faith. I tried to find answers to why this would happen to me twice in one year, but there were no answers. My personality told me I could handle everything myself. I was always self-sufficient and didn't rely on other people to help me. It was not that I didn't appreciate the offers, but I just didn't accept them. I accepted my fate as something I had to live with. I didn't dwell on it. I tried to keep my thoughts in other directions and think of happy memories. It's also not in my makeup to cry. I have never been a tearful person.

I did not read books nor did I go to grieving groups. Those first few years were lonely. However, I was and still am very active in my community doing work at the community hospital and participating in the woman's club and dance club. I retired from government work after 32 years.

But the one thing that kept me going at first was my sorority, Beta Sigma Phi, which I have been a member of for 30 years. When Susan died, people from all these other organizations sent me lots of mail, but it was my sorority sisters that I turned to. This sorority is a cultural, service and social organization and has chapters all over the world. If something like this happens, they are there for you in every respect. At the funeral they brought two huge baskets of flowers and presented me with a yellow rose, the symbol of the sorority. They were there to cook meals and do whatever needed to be done. They always offered their help in any way I needed. They were my support group and my grief group. I didn't always accept all the help offered, but I knew they cared and that was very comforting.

After three years passed my other daughter, Sharon, encouraged me to get involved in singles activities. Hesitant at first, I finally went with a girlfriend. One night I met a nice gentleman, John, who was a widower, and it will soon be six years that we've been dating. We travel together, go on cruises, attend sporting events, see movies, go to theater performances, attend dinner dance groups and do whatever else we find that's entertaining. We both have our own place to live, but we enjoy each other's company very much.

I know that I am not the normal grieving person, and I don't mean to sound harsh or cold about my recovery, but I believe that if you keep your mind and body busy, you will be able to function again sooner than you think. I did not sit around. I kept going, got active in different organizations and didn't feel sorry for myself. My religion, my sorority friends and the organizations I belong to were the essence of my recovery.

Observations of Maryanne

As Maryanne points out, she is not a typical grieving parent. She prefers to handle her own problems in her own way. This does not mean that how she has gone on with her life is wrong in any respect. Everyone grieves differently, and if she chooses not to share her grief with many people, that is her choice and others should not look down on that.

In this process she is aware of what she needs for herself to survive. Who we are tells us what we need in life. In Maryanne's case she knew exactly how she would react because it is the way she has reacted to crisis her entire life.

Having choices in our lives is what makes us survivors. Maryanne chose the opportunity to move forward with her life in a self-sufficient way. This takes courage and persistence. Some say that when we have already come through the worst thing that can happen to us, what worse thing can we fear? Perhaps that is Maryanne's philosophy. Her ability to take her life in her own hands and accept what cards have been dealt to her is Maryanne's strength. Her new life with John has been one of the positives.

For her entire life Maryanne has tackled problems using this "keep busy" approach and has survived the loss of two of the most important people in her life. I'm sure singer Frank Sinatra would agree with Maryanne. She did it "her way."

13

Stacy

"It wasn't until 20 years after my daughter died that through my volunteer work I realized I hadn't grieved and was in limbo within myself. I had done some grief for my daughter, but there was no closure because I didn't know what that meant. When I got into Reiki, everything came together...mind, body and spirit..."

Susan

I accepted everything about my daughter, no matter the problem, no matter the birth defect. It just didn't matter what was wrong with her. She was my daughter, and I loved her more than anything. Stacy turned out to be my greatest teacher, and my spiritual counselor was my validation for everything that happened those eight months that she lived in 1977.

Stacy was born with Klippel Fiel Anomalies, a combination of physical defects: vertebrae was fused in her neck; she was missing some ribs; and she had a clef pallet. All along the doctors kept saying they could do surgery when she was older, and she'd be fine. What they didn't realize was that her rib cage did not expand as her lungs grew. Her breathing became more shallow as the months went by because the lungs couldn't expand. Fluids built up in the lungs, and she died of pneumonia.

Back in 1977 little was known about the disease, yet, ironically, when my other daughter, Peggy, became pregnant four years ago, it was on the pregnancy questionnaire so they must know more about it now. I now have a granddaughter.

I did not know about the defect before she was born. The ultrasound could not detect it. I ended up having a caesarean section. She couldn't come through the birth canal because of the position of her head. I did, however, get to take her home after the birth. That was not to last. At one month the pediatrician sent me to a well-known university medical center, as he had little knowledge of her condition. At three months old Stacy had eczema all over her scalp and body. They tried everything to help her, internal and external medicines. She was taking so much medication which, I believe, affected her own immune system. Nothing seemed to help, and it just got worse. I tried to make appointments with doctors, but I was treated as an overreacting parent. Finally I said, "I'm bringing her in; something is really wrong here." When I took her in they realized she had a staph infection and was admitted to the hospital and put in quarantine. This was when I took doctors off the pedestal. It cleared up, and I once again took her home, but the eczema reappeared. We battled with it for the rest of her life.

The last three or four weeks of her life she stopped eating. She was so weak she couldn't even cry. Again, I called for appointments. They patronized me and put me off, and again I took her to the hospital without their consent. This time she never came home. She died one week later.

This was a very rare birth defect. I had an overwhelming feeling at four months that she wouldn't live long. Doctors repeatedly said, "No, she'll be okay."

I went to a spiritual counselor because this feeling I had was so strong, and I needed to talk about it. The counselor was great. She said she would tell me the truth. I gave her Stacy's name and she went into a trance. The counselor seemed to know she was ill and that she was not going to live long. In this trance she began shaking and holding her chest because she was having trouble breathing. She was very cold. Not surprising to me, that was exactly what my baby went through when she died. Stacy was put in an oxygen tent for breathing and pure oxygen is very cold. This spiritual counselor felt everything my baby felt when she died.

It validated my feelings and helped me cope. Stacy seemed to be in constant discomfort and pain, but the doctors said, "No, you're wrong, she's not in pain." They refused to even consider the possibility.

Stacy was my greatest teacher. The only way I could hold her for her comfort was with my hand behind her back as she sat in my lap facing me. She was awake a lot because of the discomfort. I would stay up with her most nights and talk to her. It was amazing. I believe she was an old soul—all knowing. It was like she was looking into my soul. It's very hard to explain, but there was a peace about her I'd never felt before.

My spiritual counselor said Stacy came back to learn one more thing: how to accept love without being able to give it. She couldn't physically put her arms out to be held and she certainly couldn't give anything back. She had a huge presence about her that I will never forget.

My husband and I dealt with our feelings about Stacy and her illness differently, and we began growing further and further apart. I realize, looking back, I was in the marriage for all the wrong reasons, and this situation made that very clear. But I had to take care of her and couldn't work, so we stayed together. We knew on some level when she died, the marriage would be over.

The one thing that kept me going was my daughter, Peggy, who was 5-years-old at the time. She was my reason for living. I had to take care of her, and that kept me moving. Peggy loved her baby sister. The last half of Stacy's life she was not up a lot; she couldn't do a lot physically. But when she was awake, Peggy would sit with Stacy and talk to her. She came to me and said, "I want you to tell me when Stacy is up; come outside and get me." She'd drop everything and stop playing, just to sit with her sister. She felt the loss tremendously, even at that young age.

In 1977 there were no support groups that I could find. I searched for emotional support as well as financial support but to no avail. Doctors' bills were unbelievable, even though we had insurance. We didn't qualify for financial support because we earned a few dollars more than allowed.

It was so hard for me to ask for help. I was raised to believe if you are truly a strong person you can do it yourself; otherwise, you are weak. I've learned much differently in the last 10 years.

I finally found the Center for Living With Dying in Santa Clara, California, and hooked up with a woman who volunteered there. I met with her many times, and she was great. She and the social worker from the hospital, who was overworked and therefore almost impossible to get together with, were the only emotional support I ever found, outside of a few family members and friends.

Later on, if I had a grief issue that was outstanding, one technique I used, say for an anniversary, was to make an appointment with myself and set aside a time where I would allow myself to grieve, to be alone with pictures, a candle, paper and pencil and allow the time for remembrance. By allowing this, it wasn't coming out in other areas of my life when I didn't want it to.

Since the death of my sister in 1970 and my husband in 1987, I realized my passion: grief and death and dying. Over the past ten years I have done volunteer work at Kaiser Hospice, at the Center For Living With Dying and at Hospice House in Monterey. I believe if I'm not able to learn and grow and ultimately share my experiences, then they were for nothing. I have been able to support others in the grief process.

This work has enabled me to understand my life better and to see the gifts my experiences have been. My dream has always been to do my own grief workshops, and that will happen very soon. I am starting my own business, and my dream is becoming a reality. It's very exciting and a little scary.

My grief workshop will be at the Reiki Center where Living With Dying used to be. I totally support the center and do volunteer work for them now. It will be a one day workshop called "The Lighter Side of Grief," to allow people to get a better understanding of what grief really is, how to grieve and the importance of grieving. We make grief difficult because we resist it. It is not socially acceptable to grieve. My work is about public education and giving people the opportunity to understand grief and how it affects their everyday life. Avoiding grief means you're making a choice not to move on with your life and you can become paralyzed. It will eventually come out in one form or another and may even manifest as physical illness. So it's really important for people to recognize their grief and allow it expression.

I've known since the late '70's that something huge was missing from my life. I didn't have a clue as to what it was. I read every self-help book I could. It wasn't until 20 years later through my volunteer work that I realized I hadn't grieved and was in limbo within myself. I had done some grief for my daughter, but there was no closure because I didn't know what that meant. When I got into Reiki, which is energy work, everything came together. That's what Reiki gives you the opportunity to do: bring mind, body and spirit to center. I now have the power in me to understand how to do "life."

An incident happened in the hospital right before Stacy died that confirmed my belief that people, on some level, know they're leaving, even little babies. A good friend flew into town to help me, and we stopped at the hospital on the way home from the airport. When I looked at Stacy, she looked back at me and put her arms up, crying like she wanted to be picked up. I was shocked she even knew who I was. A nurse whom I had never seen before was sitting there and said to me, "Do you want to hold her?" I couldn't believe it. They'd never let me hold her before. I said, "Yes," and after undoing all the connections to the equipment, I picked her up.

She looked at me the whole time, crying, not in pain, but as if she were trying to tell me something. After a few minutes she started gasping for air so I put her down. She continued to keep her arms up and cry for me. She died later that night. To this day I believe the nurse in the room was an angel. And Stacy was telling me good-bye and that everything was okay. It was an amazing experience.

I feel in my heart that grief workshops are what I am meant to be doing with my life. I'm not sure exactly the road I'll take, but if it's truly what I was meant to do, then everything will work out. There is so much information and so many aspects of grief I can teach to others.

Observations of Susan

Mothers have an uncanny way of knowing exactly about their child's health and in Susan's case, it was gratifying to have the head of pediatrics realize it when he said to her "You knew all the time, didn't you?" "Yes," said Susan. The doctor was surprised. He had no clue how she could have known that her daughter was dying. All the doctors kept reiterating until the day Stacy died was that she would be fine. Obviously, said Susan, they had never been mothers and never would be!

Hospice, which Susan worked for, is a comprehensive program of care to patients and families facing a life threatening illness or a limited life expectancy. It provides physicians, nurses, social workers, counselors, clergy and therapists for 90 percent of its patients. Families are included in the care plan. Some patients live in nursing homes or hospice centers. In most cases, insurance covers this care, but they will provide for anyone who cannot pay. After the death, Hospice provides continuing contact and support for caregivers. There are also bereavement and support groups.

Working with the Reiki Center, Susan has learned how to embrace life. Reiki is an ancient Japanese hands-on healing modality. It is Universal Life Energy. Reiki means soul power. It reminds us of our ability to heal ourselves and works on the premise that each one of us knows more about what is necessary for our healing than anyone else. It is a natural and safe method of healing and can be learned by anyone age 6 to 106.

Working with the Center for Living with Dying, whose staff counsels anyone in need, Hospice and now a Reiki practitioner, Susan has come full circle to understand the meaning of her life and her purpose here on earth. And it was all because of a small baby who came into her life for a very short but meaningful time, a child who taught Susan about unconditional love.

14

Marie

"I work through my grief in the books I write and find that keeping a journal helps too…I can tell my innermost thoughts as a release mechanism and go back to examine those feelings…"

Lauraine

We are a family of faith. God knows best even though we don't always agree with what he does. That is what my husband and I believe got us through the death of our daughter Marie, at age 21, in 1986. She died of bone cancer.

Marie was a determined and stubborn young lady when she was diagnosed at 15 years old with Ewings Sarcoma, a form of children's bone cancer. We were stunned. How could this happen to our full of life, beautiful girl? An active participant in school activities, she was well-liked and very athletic. Even though her great love was volleyball, her hip started bothering her a lot after she'd been bashed into really hard at a softball game. We thought the hip swelling stemmed from that incident. But after an x-ray, a tumor was found. The biopsy told us it was malignant.

We did whatever we could for her. At first her anger came, but then her determination took over. She believed she could beat the disease. That was how she attacked life in general. Chemo and radiation were both immediately started after the biopsy. Marie alternated treatments in the hospital and then the doctor's office every three weeks. She didn't always feel well, but she was determined to play the sport she loved no matter what. And play she did, even when she went out on the court, felt sick from the chemo, ran off the court to throw up and immediately returned to the play court to continue the game.

We made pleasure trips out of going to the hospital. She knew she'd be throwing up a few hours later, so we tried to find something fun to do to make that day less of a bummer. My philosophy is to try to celebrate every little thing because you never know what tomorrow may bring. I've always lived that way, but now I know how critical it is.

Marie went into remission and doctors said if she lived five years free of the disease she was considered cured. At five years we celebrated that she was all right, but two months later the disease came back with a vengeance and within five months Marie died.

Living with the disease was hard, but nothing compared to what it was like after Marie's death. We had continued in denial, thinking that she would make it through again. But the night she got off the airplane in California to see a specialist, I knew what was happening. Within a short time she was incoherent. You're never prepared for someone you love to die, and it's just as hard as any other kind of death.

Our friends prayed for Marie and for us. They were very supportive through the entire ordeal. That really helped us start the healing process. But I often feel gypped. I will never enjoy my only daughter's marriage, any grandchildren and all the pleasures you look forward to later in life with a daughter. We will never go shopping, out to lunch on a warm spring day or talk forever on the telephone.

The only grieving book I liked was called ***How To Survive the Loss of a Love*** by Melba Colgrove. What helped the most was my own writing.

I started writing in 1980, and a few years after Marie died, poured my heart into it full time. I realized in 1989 if I didn't go back to writing full time I'd go nuts. I took six months off from my job at a retirement home, knowing if I didn't make it as a writer, I would have to go back to work full time. Six months later I had one series going and one non-fiction book. I continued working part-time but then found I couldn't do both any more and quit my job.

I now have 39 published books and many articles that have been in magazines on a variety of subjects from business to grieving. One of the grieving articles is called *Four Gifts for Grievers* and it has been reprinted many times. The four topics I touch on in this article are (1) look beyond the statement "I am fine." Those who are grieving are not fine; (2) don't be embarrassed when you see me cry, cry with me; (3) share time and listen to what I say; (4) give the gift of touch. Touching someone is an important form of communicating. This article was a product of what I went through.

My books are contemporary and historical romances; historical family sagas; two non-fiction books on starting your own business after 50, 60 or 70, and 100 good things that happen as you grow older. In addition there are horse books for young girls, two series of 9-10 books each. In a couple of books in the series I dealt with a parent dying and how the child handled it. Counselors use those particular books as a grief tool for kids. I will continue to have death and grief as part of my fiction but do not plan to do any non-fiction books dealing with grieving. All these books I sold on my own. I have just recently gotten an agent to help me with a new book project.

I work through my grief in the books I write and find that keeping a journal helps too, even though my journal keeping is very sporadic. In those journals I can tell my innermost thoughts as a release mechanism and go back to examine those feelings. I didn't do the journaling right away. Counselors and friends kept saying to do it, and I said I would. It started with a letter to Marie. I then journaled for quite a while. Why don't I do it consistently? I should, but I don't.

I also teach and speak at writing conferences across the nation on the topics of fiction, non-fiction, marketing and whatever is needed. In addition, I do coaching, editing and encouraging types of things at the conferences. I have spoken at women's retreats, churches and businesses. In order to keep up with my writing schedule, I have had to cut back on some of that, though.

How do I find time to do all this? I don't! I don't clean house; my husband takes care of that and errands. I still enjoy yard work, but a lot of stuff other people do, such as watch TV, I don't have time for. It's not like it's a punishment. I like what I do.

Grief can tear families apart. One reason so many families split up is because so much of a mother's time is involved with the sick child. We always tried to keep the whole family involved as much as possible so the other kids didn't feel shut out. If our children had been younger it would have been different, but all were in high school when this happened to Marie. There were still times when the boys must have felt it was taking so much time away from them, although they never said so. Marie handled so much of it herself, it wasn't like taking care of a small child that demands all the time, all the energy.

My husband was supportive all the way as much as he could be. Everybody grieves in his own way, but I have found through my experience that grieving is completely different for men. Many men hide from it. They stuff it down way inside themselves, and later on it can cause severe problems, even health issues. I know because I have lived with this. If men are willing to go through the pain, then it's not as bad for any family member.

I want those who are going through the loss of a child to know five important things that I learned from all this. First, turn to God. He won't take the grieving away. He holds you up during this time and will help you to move forward. Second, don't turn away from other people. Let them help you if you need it. Reach out. Find someone who will listen. There will never be any sense to what happened, but keep talking it out. Third, understand there is a process for grieving that everyone needs to go through before you start the rest of your life. Fourth, learn what's normal. I finally sought professional help. That's when I learned what grieving was really like. Lastly, join grief organizations. There you will find companionship and understanding. I didn't join Compassionate Friends. We were moving to California, and I was working full time. Grieving took so much energy, and I didn't have any more energy to do anything. This is the order of importance I would put this in. For others, it might be a different order.

When I think of my daughter, I work at thinking of the good times. It has become a lot easier through the years. The pain is still there but nothing like it was. The memories are there. I live through the memory, feel the feeling and get beyond it and go on from there. If you dwell in the sorrow, it will drag you down. Yet, if you don't feel it when it comes, it will latch on forever. Wallowing in it doesn't help. If you feel and not try to 'not' feel it, it will go away faster.

Sometimes it all comes back and grabs you and you are caught in a flood of tears. But that is okay. She will be with me always. I sometimes think to myself, "I got through this loss; I can get through anything!"

Observations of Lauraine

Lauraine keeps very busy these days with all her writing, speaking and teaching. She is doing what she loves, yet it is also a way to deal with her loss. Many parents have a hard time verbally expressing to others their true feelings and may find it easier to write them down and look back at these writings hours, days, months and years later to see how far they have come. Lauraine used her journaling as a way to "tell her innermost thoughts as a release mechanism and go back to examine those feelings." Real growth can come out of these expressions of loss, out of feeling your feelings, whether those feelings are ones of sadness, rage, vengeance or guilt. By expressing what is deep within, it allows you to move forward with your life and may, in turn, allow you to deal successfully with yourself, surviving family members and friends.

Others may want to keep a daily diary of exactly what happened during the first year. Diaries may be the only way you will remember after the shock subsides, and you may find it a good way to measure your progress. What you write one day may show marked improvement over what you wrote months before. A daily diary makes it easier to see when the healing process begins. Getting better does not mean that you didn't love your loved one enough, are being disloyal or that you will forget him or her. When and how you begin to feel better is up to you.

Lauraine also keeps lots of pictures of Marie around the house. The family talks about her life, but other than that there are no celebrations, no memorials, no remembrances. She is remembered in their hearts; her courage is a symbol of what they all strive for; and Marie is no doubt busy, trying to find a team for the next volleyball match.

15

Brian

> *"When I don't hear people say, 'I miss Brian' I am very sad. Those who knew him...will talk about him, but most will not. I received support when I needed it, but I don't believe there is enough of it out there for most..."*
>
> Nat

I found my 24 year old son, Brian, dead in 1995 when I went to his apartment one day after not being able to contact him. How he died was undetermined. No autopsy was done after an intensive investigation by the N.Y.P.D. I found, under New York law, an autopsy is not required if there is not an element of foul play.

Some may find it strange that my wife, Fern, and I did not order the autopsy. My feeling was it wasn't important at the time to know 'why' he died. It was bad enough just knowing he was dead. My wife and I both felt comfortable with our decision since we knew Brian to be in good health and to this day the thought of an autopsy never enters our mind.

I have some feelings about the cause of his death. Brian was into nutrition; he was a body builder, and I have read articles about people his age who took over-the-counter supplements with bad reactions. He also could have choked on something. He was found lying near the toilet.

Brian, an individualist who marched to his own drum, was finishing law school at the time of his death. He did receive his degree posthumously. Like a chameleon, he would change his colors to whatever suited him. He had many interests. One minute he could recite Shakespeare, the next he could watch Star Trek. Being an avid reader, poetry, the classics and science fiction all interested him. He loved all types of outdoor adventures such as mountain climbing, parachuting and repelling. Things came easy for him, and he did what he liked, when he liked. His happiest times were in seeing others happy. He had a heart as big as the sea and a hand that was always extended to help those who needed help, whether he knew them or not.

He chose to be an individual, a non-conformist in an environment that stressed conformity. His appearance was unlike others in the clothes he wore and the way he styled his hair, possibly making a statement and challenging others to also be individuals. Brian had that unique quality to be a spark that could ignite the best in all with whom he came in contact. He could make you laugh and he could make you angry. He dug deeply into other's hearts encouraging them to recognize their best qualities.

In school Brian was involved with adaptive aquatics. This is a method used to help the mentally and physically handicapped through swimming. He did his undergraduate work at Stony Brook University and spent a lot of time in this area. He was always sensitive to others not as fortunate as he. In particular he worked with an autistic and deaf boy for three years that no one else could reach. He communicated with him through self-taught sign language. Brian was the only person this boy showed any affection to and after three years, the boy was comfortable in the water. An instructional tape was made of this program and sold to many universities across the United States. The tape was dedicated to Brian.

A memorial award was also set up by the university's Adaptive Aquatics Program in memory of Brian for those in the university program who achieved the highest standards of adaptive aquatics. What's nice for us is that it was given after he left the university. The kids getting the award didn't know Brian, but they knew what he did, and this was a standard set for those very serious about their work. People who receive the award have gotten to know him because of winning it. We got involved in the university program, too, by contributing to the program as did many of our friends and relatives.

When Brian died I can only describe my feelings as being very, very empty and very sad. I have one other son, two years younger, who got along great with Brian. Not a day goes by I don't spend time with Brian, visualizing him. I do a lot of different things during each day that remind me of him. He is in my first thoughts as I wake in the morning. If I see other kids nowadays, I wonder what Brian would be like now. Where would he be? Thousands of things happen during the day that bring him to mind. Sometimes they are sad thoughts, sometimes not. But they never go away.

At first I also felt anger towards Brian. He was at a point of maturity where he had almost graduated and was well on his way to becoming a successful lawyer. I believe he might have let himself down, not that he had the power to change the circumstances.

But for the most part it was pain that I felt. I tried to be as realistic as I could under the circumstances. I coped by going back to work immediately, an office supply business. I didn't hide my emotions. I talked about it to anyone who would listen in the working environment. There were a few that listened and were supportive, but I immediately recognized a lot of people didn't really care to know. I even found that some customers didn't come back after they heard what happened. At first I was angry, but soon realized that's the way life is, and whatever reason they had, that was something I couldn't control.

A couple of months after Brian's death, a customer of mine was talking about his two girls. He was very proud of them and spoke about their accomplishments. "How about you?" he said to me. I told him my oldest son had recently died. He said "Oh, my God. I feel so bad for talking as I did. I can't imagine how you feel. I'm so sorry I babbled about my daughters." It was nice that someone felt sympathy and concern. Two weeks later, though, that same customer came back and said "Hi, Nat, how's your boys?"

Time goes by, tomorrow comes whether you're sad or happy. My thoughts remain: this is life. I don't expect others to feel the emptiness, the sadness, as I do.

My wife and I became active in The Compassionate Friends about three months after Brian died. We found it extremely helpful for us to be with people who went through the same thing. We didn't feel alone and still attend meetings to hopefully help others. I look forward to being with these people. We have come to know people who didn't go to bereavement groups, and I feel they haven't healed, that a group such as this one would have been beneficial to them.

Functioning again was a gradual, continual process. I found the second year rougher than the first. It wasn't until the end of the second year that I didn't feel guilty if I laughed at a joke or if I was enjoying myself. During these first years I couldn't do anything Brian liked and enjoy it. I couldn't read science fiction or poetry. We had done that together.

When I don't hear people say "I miss Brian," I am very sad. Those who knew him growing up or from school will talk about him, but most will not. I received support when I needed it, but I don't believe there is enough of it out there for most. At our Compassionate Friends meetings one topic we talk about at every meeting is the attitude of others towards us.

I try to tell those who are just starting the grief process that things get better as time goes on. I don't think they believe it when I tell them. They have to heal themselves, but I will give them support as best as possible.

Brian left us in 1995 a few weeks before springtime, just as the roots of all the world's beauty had taken hold in the flowers that bloom and the trees that blossom. Perhaps Brian, too, sprinkled his own seeds of beauty upon us as he traveled through his life's experiences so we too can blossom and bloom, rededicating ourselves to making this world a better place.

Observations of Nat

When a child dies you want to know why. For most, it is a prerequisite to grieving. For Nat, it was a question that didn't need an answer. His son was dead. An autopsy wasn't needed. Nothing would bring him back. The reason he died didn't matter. It was the right decision at the time, according to Nat. I can appreciate how he feels, but for many, they must know every detail of the circumstances of death. Everyone must do what they feel works for them. There is no right or wrong answer to this situation. According to Nat it wouldn't have changed anything.

At Compassionate Friends meetings Nat says a constant topic is the attitude of others towards the bereaved parent. Others need to know you want to talk about your child. When they don't, it compounds what you have lost; it makes you feel like your child didn't matter. Bereaved parents say if you talked about a child when he was alive, then talk about him after he dies. He will always be in their hearts and thoughts.

Like these parents, Nat wants to remember his son, but feels that others, for whatever reason they may have, over the years, talk about his son less and less. It is his worst fear. We are all afraid the memory will fade if we don't talk about our children. It won't. What we eventually realize is that unless others walk in our shoes and know our pain, they can not suffer with us. As time passes, our pain is still there while others have moved on, some having given support and some not. To understand this is an important recovery step. Nat knows and accepts this as part of life.

16

Eric

> *"As a nurse…one of my jobs was to offer comfort to those who lost children. As a survivor myself, I found I could empathize in a way another person never could…"*
>
> Sally

When your child dies you find out who your true friends are. We found this out in 1989 when our first child was stillborn.

Those you think will be the most help during a time like this weren't terribly supportive. They weren't there for us to talk to, and they didn't understand. Even if they had a relative die, it's not the same as having a child die.

I was also offended by what some people said, thoughtless statements like "Well, you can have another one, let us know when the next baby shower is" or "When are you going to try again?" as though it was no big deal. One friend wished me a Merry Christmas; Mel was off to the Gulf War as a medical technician, and my child had been dead only a few months!

My best friend at the time seeing me crying and unhappy all the time told me that if I didn't get over this, my husband was going to leave me. I never spoke to her again.

I am a nurse, and it was our medical friends who were the most helpful even though they, too, were at a loss for words. Other supportive friends came to us and asked if they could be there for us when our second son was born, and they were.

Once you can learn to accept the fact of how differently people react, you can distinguish between those who are just plain rude and those who mean well but can't express it.

Eric died when I was in labor. Everything was perfect, but during the birth, the baby's skull was molded in such a way as he came through the birth canal that he compressed his brain stem which in turn stopped his heart. It happened in one minute.

At first everyone thought one of the machines had malfunctioned; it was unbelievable that such a simple delivery could go so wrong. When they realized it was not the machines, they tried to resuscitate the baby but couldn't. Doctors said this occurrence was very rare, one in a million. When asked what the chances were that it happen again, doctors said they could not know.

We're sorry his organs couldn't be saved for donation, but it was too late.

The baby was washed, wrapped in a blanket and brought to us so we could hold it. Pictures were taken as well as footprints. We believe it's important for parents to see their children, even after they die, so they always have something to remember. We're sorry we didn't spend more time with him. A memorial service was held at the hospital.

Because it was so unexpected for the baby to die, a funeral was planned, but today we believe they should have cremated him so he could always be with us. Nowadays, I believe it is especially important to cremate if the family is in the military and moves around a lot. It is difficult to go to the cemetery if you are thousands of miles away. I'm lucky. My in-laws live in the city where the baby is buried and can bring flowers on different occasions and holidays.They go about four times a year. My parents go also and help to keep it clean. My wish is still to one day cremate Eric if possible.

Initially, we were in deep shock. We expected to leave the hospital and go home with a healthy baby. But here I was at home, still wearing maternity clothes because of the weight gain, but feeling empty inside. I thought one day I would wake up and find out everything was okay. That, of course, didn't happen.

We went through the grief process, quietly spent a lot of time at the grave site at first, and even saw a psychologist for five sessions to speed up the healing process, but then Mel got sent to the Gulf during the war. I thought the sessions helped, but Mel was not that interested, and so we never went again after he returned. And, of course, I realized that you never completely heal from a child's death; you just accept what has happened and move on with your life as best as you can.

I have dealt with the deaths of three grandparents and other relatives and was involved with their funerals, while Mel has never experienced a close death. I think that made it all the more difficult for him. He is not a very open person, keeps a lot bottled up inside and, even to this day, doesn't share the loss of our child with others unless it is brought up.

What helped the most for both of us was time. The nursery was left up for about six weeks and finally everything placed in boxes. We would go in there and just cry. Even after we took it down, while Mel was at work, I would still go in there and cry if I felt like it. This went on for almost a year.

I now keep a box by my bed with a lock of Eric's hair, cards I received, his baby footprints, a poem called "The Borrowed Child" and some shower items. On his birthday I take it all out, look at it and read the poem.

The first year I tried to work on his birthday, April 29, but I couldn't make it through the day, so now I just take off every year on that day. It's just too hard for me to even concentrate.

As a nurse, in addition to prenatal teaching, one of my jobs while we lived in Texas was to offer comfort to those who lost children. As a survivor I found I could empathize in a way another person never could. This helped me in the healing process.

I also read a few books, the best of which was ***When Bad Things Happen to Good People*** by Harold Kushner. I always had to carry a tissue with me when reading it. It was that emotional for me.

What I tell people who have to go through this experience is that you'll find out who your friends are and not to be offended by what some say.

The joy of our life, our second child, Quinn, was born a few years later. Everything turned out fine in the labor and delivery room, but it was a tense time, knowing the worst could happen again.

Quinn knows about Eric and that he is in heaven watching over him and the entire family.

Observations of Sally

This couple seems to have had more trouble dealing with other people's reactions than most of those interviewed. Most grieving parents would prefer others just to be there for them. They don't need to say anything, just be supportive. Knowing how much people care and understand the hurt can help others put their lives back together. But there are those who don't call or come around. To them it never happened. It is almost like they are afraid to face the reality of someone dying. Those who say things like "you need to forget" or "it was for the best" may not mean any harm and simply may not have been taught any differently, and it is up to us to distinguish between cruelty and ignorance. No matter how short their lives or how little chance parents have to know them, the children were real. So when parents encounter friends or family who don't respond to the loss in a way that the parents feel is appropriate, rifts occur.

For parents, a stillborn child or one who dies during or shortly after birth is still real and intensely important. Keeping remembrances from the child that they can look at for the rest of their lives is a comfort and a good healing tool.

Organizations such as Empty Cradle in San Diego speak to the need of connecting with people who have been there. The group also speaks to hospital staffs, making them aware of a parent's fears during pregnancy, delivery and shortly afterwards. Respect for a parent's grief in the hospital and a confirmation that the baby was a real person show that staff members empathize, which is appreciated by parents. Many parents continue to work for Empty Cradle as a facilitator, talking by phone with newly bereaved parents.

17

Paul

"Why had God done this to me? I hated Him. I hated myself...I looked at God as out there somewhere, not in my heart...It took many years to understand that God is loving, not vengeful. God lives within me and everyone..."

Barbara

What has gotten me through is my faith in God. God did not punish me. He is a loving God. Knowing that He helps me to handle all the peaks and valleys in my life is comforting.

But when Paul died, you could not convince me of that. I went through a lot of guilt, especially with the knowledge that I did not want to be pregnant at the time and that I had never gotten to even see or hold him.

I was a young mother with an 18-month old active boy, a 9-month old baby girl and a husband still in school. Another child at this point was not what I had envisioned although there was no question in my mind: I would not have an abortion. Neither did I anticipate how difficult the pregnancy would be. There was much pain and swelling of the joints and most of the time I didn't feel good. At the beginning of my eighth month a baby boy, 4 pounds, 3 ounces was born. Paul had a lot of mucus and, as a result, was to be kept in the nursery those five days I was hospitalized. The doctor said he was doing much better the second day, and I would get to see, hold and feed him the morning of the third day. But during the night, a nurse woke me up and said the doctor wanted to see me.

The doctor said he was not doing well. His brain had hemorrhaged and there was very little chance for survival. If he did survive, he would probably be a vegetable. By the time I called my husband, Denis, and he arrived at the hospital, Paul was gone. I had never seen him.

The funeral was held while I was still in the hospital. My husband, Denis, arranged everything. I convinced myself I was handling it well. I didn't have to face reality yet. Take care of your other children, get into your normal routine, I told myself. Don't let yourself get upset.

But when I got home the walls went up and started closing in on me. I couldn't cry. I was numb. I was a robot, functioning but not feeling. Nobody could reach me. Friends and relatives tried to give support and friendship, but I just wanted them to go away and leave me alone. My mother didn't help either when she would continually say things like "how terrible to lose my grandchild." At one point I even had to ask her to leave the house and go home. Denis tried to give me the space I needed, as if he understood that I would eventually work it out myself. I sometimes think back, knowing he did all the funeral arrangements and burial without me, and wonder how he got through it.

Denis was the type that kept everything in. We didn't talk about Paul much until years later. Because he had been in the priesthood for a time before we met, I knew he took everything that happened as God's will. "God needed him more than we did," he believed. It was not that he was not sad or distraught at the time. He was just more able to handle it because of his religious beliefs.

But not me. Why had God done this to me? I hated Him. I hated myself. Sometimes I even tried to convince myself the whole thing had not happened. I looked at God as out there somewhere, not in my heart. I felt unworthy.

Two weeks after I got home friends invited us out for the evening. I didn't want to go anywhere. I didn't want to see anyone. My husband thought it would be good for me and insisted we go. I remember feeling very uncomfortable. Everyone was looking at me, trying to assess my reactions and feelings. I was out of my comfort zone. I felt like I was in a room of strangers rather than long time friends. The music playing was annoying me. The conversation felt stifling. It felt like I was going crazy. I finally got out of my seat and walked out without saying anything to anyone.

Something happened to me that night. Maybe it was being around other women who were living normal happy lives with their husbands and children. Or maybe it was hearing them tell me how their son or daughter was going to be in the school play. Or the next family vacation. Or maybe it was just the way they looked or spoke to me, trying to be jovial and carefree, but very careful about what they said. All I know is that I started to cry when I got home and continued to cry all night and the next day. I thought the tears would never stop. I cried for Paul, for all the years I would miss seeing him grow up; for my other children, who would never know their brother; and for Denis, who could never play baseball with his son in the back yard.

And when the tears finally stopped it was like I had begun to cleanse myself and my heart began to open. I knew I couldn't dwell on the negative. I had to go on. There were other children involved. I buried myself in work. When I wasn't working I was busy taking the children to friends or school activities. I kept busy all the time. That way I didn't have to think about what I had lost. It would take many years to work through the guilt, the hate, the feelings associated with losing Paul, but I was able to do what at one time I thought impossible. I also came to realize my feelings were normal reactions associated with the death of a child and that nothing I could have done would have changed the outcome.

After Paul's death I became pregnant with twins who died before they were born, and I went through an additional miscarriage the following year. Only three of my seven children lived. I think by Paul's death, the first, God was preparing me to be able to cope with the other deaths later on.

I became active in church and its activities. It took many years to understand that God is loving, not vengeful. God lives within me and everyone. We're part of the same body. When you die, the number of people you have loved in your life will be with you when you die.

Paul was born in 1967, and not a day passes that I don't think of him. What would he have been like as he grew up? Would he have been tall, short, skinny, heavyset, handsome? Would the girls have been crazy about him? What would he have been interested in? Perhaps an athlete? Or a scientist? I will never know, but those thoughts never leave my mind. One thing I did learn. The number of years your child is dead never changes how you feel and you never, never forget them. And why should you? I just wish I had some memories to keep within me, but there are none.

When I hear of someone I know who has lost a child or any loved one, I try to just be there for them. I know how it feels. Words are not necessary. Just open arms and a caring heart will hopefully help to ease their pain.

It is especially hard for me during the holidays or special occasions, although time has a way of easing the pain that never leaves you. But at a Christmas dinner or on Paul's birthday my mind is always there with him. My three children are all grown and gone from home, and I am a grandma of four beautiful grandchildren. For years I was active with the youth group of my church, but I know now when I retire I want to do volunteer work in a children's hospital where I can rock the babies who have no one and give them the love they deserve.

I know that God has really blessed me, and I am sure my time will come, not in this life, when I will someday be able to hold Paul in my arms. We walk this walk but once, and we have to hold on to all the gifts God gives us. If he sees fit to take home those we love prematurely, we have to go on. This doesn't mean forgetting, because a mother can never forget. We need to be able to accept all he gives us, the joys, the pains, the growth and his love.

Paul will always be my special child, my little angel, and I know without a doubt one day we will be together again in heaven.

Observations of Barbara

Even though it took time to realize, it was her religion and her belief in God and all the good He does that helped Barbara get through her infant son's death and three miscarriages. God gave her strength, hope and courage to deal with the pain and loss and survive the tragedy. God did not cause the tragedy, nor should He be blamed. When she thought she was alone, she realized God was by her side as were her family and friends, helping her to handle whatever was necessary.

Barbara understands no one can escape death if it is one's time to go. And she believes that God has his reasons for taking good people, and we are not to judge that reason. More good things happen to us than bad. She also knows that before you can feel joy, you must know sorrow, and so she was burdened with four deaths, but blessed with three children and four grandchildren. She considers herself lucky. Everyone is healthy, and she is a devoted mother and grandmother. She knows it is because she has led a good life filled with kindness, tolerance, generosity and above all, love for others and God.

Each person must decide for himself whether a spiritual connection will help in recovery.

18

Gary

> *"I tried so hard to talk to my son, to get him help when he was diagnosed with diabetes...We did everything we could possibly do to support him. But he would have none of it. He hated his life and eventually ended it...I am not guilt ridden...I did what I could..."*
>
> Bernadine

If I could say something to my son now that he is gone, it would be, "Gary, I know you're at peace because you don't have to take any more shots for your diabetes." For his sake, I'm glad he's not here. The diabetes killed him, not physically, but emotionally.

My son, Gary, committed suicide when he was 25 years old in 1992. It was something I could see coming, but you keep telling yourself you should never think those thoughts. Could I have saved him? I know now I couldn't. He couldn't even save himself in the end.

I tried so hard to talk to him, to get him help when, at 13, he was diagnosed with Type I Diabetes and had to take insulin shots three times a day. I believe the divorce I was going through at the time brought it out early, but he would more than likely have gotten it later. The stress was very bad for him. He was a high strung kid, but a good one.

We did everything we could possibly do to support him. But he would have none of it. He didn't want to talk about it. He hated his life. He said it every day. He couldn't accept the diabetes as an illness with which it was possible to live a complete life. He believed he was the only one in the world that had to suffer as he did. The fact that he had wanted to be a pilot all his life, but couldn't because of the diabetes, didn't help.

"I wish I wasn't here," I remember him saying often.

"You need help," I would tell him. "Let us help you or at least let us get help for you."

In California where he was a paralegal we got him into the City of Hope treatment center. Besides a well-known cancer center they have a wonderful diabetes section and psychiatrists that could talk to him and help him learn to live with the disease. Gary would go there now and then to regulate his blood sugar, but he wouldn't let me talk to the doctors.

"You need a support group. Please go."

"Why should I? Who's going to want me with this disease?"

He would never go. I begged and begged.

"No, I won't go so quit asking me! I won't go back at all if you interfere," he told me. And so I didn't. I hoped what we did for him at home, as a family, would be enough. It wasn't.

When we would go to a restaurant to eat, he didn't want to take the insulin with him. I had to carry it. He was totally ashamed to have to take insulin, completely non-accepting of the disease. Because he didn't take care of himself, a few times he landed in the hospital due to the high levels and he would say, "I'll never be able to take the shots."

I don't know if he overreacted with the shots because he was afraid he'd lose a limb or his eyesight, which are common results from complications. He worried about things before they happened and overreacted to everything. He would not let anyone see him get a shot and would never talk about the disease. He was ashamed. "Why am I like this?" he would ask.

He became very quiet when he was moody. "What's the matter?" I would ask him. "Leave me alone!" he would say. He didn't want me to tell him what to do.

The diabetes didn't allow him to think straight. He was paranoid. After graduating from Hunter College with a degree in political science and moving to California near his parents, he would say, "I'm so tired, I want to go to sleep, but I have to stay up for a snack so the diabetes will stay level."

When he jumped nine stories from the Santa Monica Mall parking garage, police asked if I thought there could be foul play. I knew there wasn't. He had done what I suspected for many weeks. And there were clues all along. Again my brain did not want to digest what Gary was saying to me and so I ignored them, relying on the adage, "Things will get better with time."

One week before, he had gotten the flu. The flu can play havoc on diabetes by raising the blood sugar tremendously. I helped him out or at least tried to during this time. I would bring food to his apartment, but he wouldn't let me in. "Just leave it," he would say. "Go away." He was verbally abusive to me during this time.

The night before he killed himself, I took him to dinner. He ordered all the things he shouldn't eat at the restaurant. I didn't say anything. I was afraid he would either get up and leave or start telling me why his life was a waste. The next day he called and met me at a deli. I noticed his unkempt appearance. He was nervous, his hair was not combed, he had the same shirt on as the night before. Usually, he was very neat. He kept getting up and down, like he was out of control. Again I begged him to go to the City of Hope and get help and, of course, again he refused. I had a bad feeling that day, but wrongly, I thought if I left him alone with his demons, he would overcome them as he had on many other occasions.

I never saw him again. Because I was so worried I kept calling. I sensed something that day different from the others. And then he didn't show up for dinner.

The Santa Monica police called at 9:30 p.m. and said they'd be right over.

"He's dead," I screamed. "I know it." And he was.

I should not have been surprised about the suicide. Gary got into Yoga when he was 19 and, from what I understand, those believing in it are not afraid to die. He also told an Indian friend he was going to jump, that he couldn't stand the disease, that life was not worth living with it. Another clue was when he said to me out of the clear blue, "If I should die before you, I don't want to wear a blue suit, and I don't want to be embalmed." Things like this come back to you when you have so much time after a death to think about their life. I remember saying at the time, "Don't tell me that. I don't want to hear you talking like this."

I couldn't go into his apartment afterwards. My husband's employees cleaned everything out. For months I walked around in a daze. I didn't cry much. It's not my nature to cry. But I always felt sick to my stomach. To this day every once in a while I get that same feeling when I hear a song, see a place we used to visit and especially when I go past the Santa Monica Mall. I have to turn away. It is still too hard and may always be.

An acquaintance called after Gary died and said she was forming a group of parents whose children committed suicide and asked me to join them. "No thanks," I told her. "It's not for me. I can work it out myself." And I eventually did.

I am not a guilt-ridden person. I do the best in my life I can for whoever I care about. Why should I feel guilty? You can only do so much. I made a decision. I had a wonderful life, three other children that needed me, a fantastic husband. I could either be miserable to my husband, who had been so good to Gary even though he was only a step-son. I could let my children see me suffer and add to their own suffering. Or I could be strong for all of them and help them survive too. This went over and over in my mind for months. Nothing I could do would bring Gary back. I had to survive and do it for everyone else.

The anger that at first engulfed me and the question "How could he do this to me and everyone who loved him so much?" dissipated. As my husband Dick said, "You never walked in his shoes. You don't know how hard it was for him."

At first I went to the cemetery a lot. I wanted to be near him, to sit with him. I knew he was at peace, and I was happy for him. But I also wanted him with me, so that we could be a whole family again. When I see his name on the stone, I get a horrible feeling. That stone is the acknowledgement that he is gone, and it's so hard to believe I'll never see him again. So I don't go much anymore. Selfishly, I'm sorry he wasn't married and didn't have any children so that a part of him would go on forever.

The knot in my stomach disappeared after about seven years. It's not as hard now. I go on with my life each day with my husband and my other children. I keep pictures of Gary around the house. I like to look at him. Sometimes when I get a gift or some flowers I place them by his picture. Such a handsome face…such a kind soul…at peace…at last.

Observations of Bernardine

Bernardine's story is not a typical one. When a child commits suicide not only is there anger on the parent's part that the child is gone and his future can not be shared, but there is usually blame and guilt that maybe if they had tried just one more thing, it could have helped. Suicide makes others uncomfortable and unwilling to talk to the grieving parents. Society tends to judge these parents unfairly.

Bernardine's reaction was free of guilt. She knew her son was hurting and as hard as she tried, nothing she did helped. She would have jumped at any opportunity to save him. Now she no longer lives in fear of what the next phone call might bring. She has already faced the worst possible thing that could happen, but because of her strength of character and her family needs, she was able to take any anger felt and lay it aside to move on with her life. She is able to concentrate on the good memories, make some sense out of her loss and smiles now when she talks about her son and his positive qualities she will always continue to remember.

If a parent can not work through the anger, guilt, blame and social stigma of a suicide, there are others who will listen to the pain. Therapists and groups such as American Society of Suicidology and The Samaritans are highly recommended.

19

Tommy and Paul Jr.

"We learned husbands and wives grieve very differently...and the medical community didn't have a clue...people had to be educated. This was done through an after-care program in trauma centers."

Bridie and Paul

When my youngest son, Tommy, 17,was killed in an automobile accident in 1985 and our oldest, Paul Jr., 23, died in a plane accident 22 months later, my husband and I had very different reactions to our only two children dying . Though we are now at the same place in our feelings, it was a very long journey to this point...Bridie

Tommy's car hit a bridge abutment, and he died instantly. I was totally unprepared for the death of my child, a shocking, devastating event. When the police came to the back door, it was every parent's nightmare. "Tommy is hurt," the policeman said. "Get to the hospital." I knew, looking at his averted eyes and his expression, that Tommy was dead. When Bridie and I got to the hospital in New Haven, the ambulance door was still opened and the two attendants also averted eye contact. Now I was sure even though no one said anything. We were ushered into a room and waited 15 minutes for anyone to show up. A woman doctor finally arrived and very coldly and quickly told us Tommy was dead. There was no caring attitude, no compassion. A Chaplain came in, mumbled something and left. We were shocked at the treatment we received, but in the midst of it, all I could feel was a great, devastating pain…Paul

Tommy was a bundle of energy. A very outgoing teen, he was class president and captain of the football team at the time of his death. All of Tommy's friends came to the emergency room. As a mom, my attention went to them. I was captured by what was going on with these kids for months. I still felt pain, but I became so involved and concerned for them, my personal grieving was put aside for a while…Bridie

There was a period of weeks when our house became a haven for Tom's friends, and I felt, after a while, I didn't want them there. I felt intruded on. It was one of the differences between Bridie and I. She took great comfort in having them there…Paul

It was at this point we were to learn how differently we all grieve, even husbands and wives. I watched the response of these kids. They were devastated; it was, for many, the first death they had experienced. The lesson I learned from them was how open kids can be. They didn't hold their grief in; they supported each other and me and tried to with Paul. They were loving and giving. I found that to be wonderful…Bridie

I went back to work after a week to pay the bills. At work, it was a double-edged sword. By having to go to work and physically leave the house (I work on a tugboat and travel a lot), I felt I had to do it. It got my mind elsewhere for a time. But a number of times I'd get halfway through a work period and then crumble. I would cry and cry. I couldn't think. Fortunately, I worked with a good, caring friend who would take over and work for me, telling me to go rest. The pain, like ground glass, starts to get dulled around the edges. Even though you're still hurting, it's not quite as sharp. I worked and as time went on, I was able to function, but it wasn't easy…Paul

I, on the other hand, didn't go back to work in nursing for three months. I didn't trust myself to make decisions dealing with people. I felt like someone had taken razor blades to my insides. I couldn't see it in the mirror, but I could see it inside me. I was amazed that Paul was able to work. I even had difficulty remembering things, including good times with Tommy. My mind just wanted to shut down, physically and emotionally.—Bridie

The funeral had a huge turnout, even though I felt like I was in a trance. My younger brother, David, who I was very close to, and my older brother, flew in for the funeral. As the casket was being taken to the hearse to go to the cemetery, David, 37 years old, keeled over and died of a massive heart attack. As we went to bury Tommy, at the same time an ambulance was in the parking lot of the church taking my brother away. Within two days Bridie and I had another funeral. I was in total disbelief that this could happen. When it wore off, the pain was so awful I can't describe it…Paul

It was almost a replay of 22 months earlier as state police came to our door when Paul Jr.'s plane went down. Again, they told Bridie and I nothing, but I had an ominous feeling. The police gave us a phone number, and we had to call Boston to find out what had happened. Then further shock and disbelief, and this time, unlike Tommy's death, an immediate and overwhelming anger at God and the pilot who survived. The pilot of the small plane Paul Jr. was in made errors in judgment that caused the crash. He had not refueled. The plane had simply run out of gas and went down in Long Island Sound. Both the pilot and Paul Jr. swam around for many hours. The pilot was eventually rescued. Paul Jr.'s body was not found for six days…Paul

Between the deaths of my sons, I was not aware of anger for quite a while. Then it was anger at God and Tommy. Then through a process before Paul Jr. died, I was just angry at the situation. When I didn't work, I read a lot about death, life after death, etc. A very big part of what happened to me was spiritual. It was always a part of my life anyway, but it became an important part of this whole process and journey. When Paul Jr. died, again Paul and I had different reactions…Bridie

Paul Jr., although outgoing, was a very quiet youngster. When little, I could sit him down, give him a book to read and four hours later come back and he'd still be there involved with the book, an exact opposite in that respect from Tommy. But the boys got along great, and Paul and I are very grateful that they were always able to say, "I love you" to each other even if they fought at times like most siblings…Bridie

Unlike Bridie, my anger turned to rage and consumed me. It's all I thought about. I was out of control, cursing God and saying I wanted something awful to happen to the pilot. But I'm grateful it didn't. I know now that left unchecked, anger and rage will undo you in every way. I had a hell of a struggle getting out from under that mess. It went on for a long, long time…Paul

What finally helped me with this anger were three things. First, joining The Compassionate Friends was the immediate help. We started a chapter in our area where there was none. It gave us something to focus our energies on. We got a good core group. The couples knew what to say, how to help. I was very active for two years and then began to phase out. Second, having two close friends was helpful. One spoke firmly and from the heart, convincing me to seek professional help. He pushed and pushed me until I finally went to a grief counselor. I connected with this counselor, liked him a lot and saw him for two years, twice a month. We talked about everything, all the deaths and my anger at God. He helped me vent that anger. Third, this may sound corny, but it's true. Time going by was a big help…Paul

I felt very different. I continued with Compassionate Friends even after Paul stopped. One time I said at a meeting, "You never think it's going to happen to you. This kind of thing happens to others. When it does happen, you realize you're not invincible and it could happen again." The next day Paul Jr. died…Bridie

I was convinced God wouldn't let this happen again. When they found his body, I didn't feel anger like my husband. In the midst of all my pain I felt, "It's right because Paul and Tommy are together; it's what they would want." To some degree this gave me comfort. From there I became interested in finding out just what this is all about. What is life about? Where is it going? These questions took me on a spiritual journey. A priest helped me in the realm of spirituality, not religion. I read a lot discovering on the way that all the religions are basically very similar, but there is a lot to discover. There is no black or white answer to what happens. But there are signs. There is a plan out there. This was meant to happen. Even at the worst of this, there were such obvious, wonderful things going on. The best was the absolute outpouring of love that continues to this day. It is unbelievable. All the love that was shown to us was a stabilizing factor for me. I couldn't have held it together without that. TCF is an important part of our life today. We wouldn't have met these wonderful people if our boys hadn't died. Paul and I are different now on a much deeper level. We aren't so caught up with worldly, material things. We don't sweat the small stuff. Life is not about the superficial. There is more to life. If these tragedies had not happened, we would have been content to go on with our materialistic world. Out of all this, there is a much deeper resonance...Bridie

Now that time has gone by, I believe there were reasons this happened, like Bridie, but it totally baffles me what those reasons are. I'm comfortable that I will know eventually, but it will not be on this earth. I have come to an acceptance of what has happened. This doesn't mean I don't miss the boys. From time to time I look at photos; sometimes I pause as I walk through the house. I still feel great sadness and loss after all this time, but now the pain is not as sharp. Sometimes without warning I see a child and the memories come. It hurts to know we'll never have grandchildren. Bridie can't go to baby showers, not because of the baby, but because of the conversation that takes place at the shower about the grandchildren. She says it's like a spear to her heart. And there is a serious fear of what will happen to us at the end of our life. We are totally alone. There is no one left to carry on the family line, to leave heirlooms to. It scares me…Paul

We still never go to the cemetery together. I don't want to add to Paul's pain or feel I have to hold my feelings in. It upsets him to see me come undone, not uncommon when I am at the cemetery…Bridie

Through all this the medical community didn't have a clue as to how we, and all parents, feel when our children die. Most don't understand the parameters of grieving, how people grieve, how long it takes and how to help with anger, like Paul's, which was a scary thing. To make sense and give meaning to what had happened to us and others, I needed to help educate people…Bridie

An after-care program in a trauma center was started 15 years ago by other mothers who were nurses who recognized this is not the way you treat people. I got involved three years ago and am now coordinator for the program in my area. This program works so well it has been picked up by trauma centers all over the country. We put workshops together and give lectures to professionals (teachers, nurses, policemen) and to local colleges. In two workshops a year we also train the volunteers who in turn help families going through a child's death or any death. The volunteers stay with the families in the trauma centers, answer questions, etc. The families can stay in this program for up to two years. If we help one person make their journey easier, then what I am doing now has been worth all the time and effort…Bridie

My husband and I are now at the same place. Before, this was not so. We had different reactions, but through it all we have always been able to talk about the boys. So even if we weren't at the same point during our grief period, it was good for us to talk to each other…Bridie

Three years ago Paul and I took our first real vacation since the boys died. We went to Hawaii, a dream of ours for many years. To be able to come from where we were with all that awfulness, heartache and despair to be able to say you thoroughly enjoyed yourself on a vacation is a real accomplishment for us…Bridie

Observations of Bridie and Paul

Bridie and Paul, through this conversation, tried very hard to show that husbands and wives may grieve differently. That is not an uncommon occurrence nor does it mean that there is anything wrong with the marriage. Men and women may be brought up differently by their parents, and this may shape how they react. If we understand how a family copes under unusual circumstances, we are more able later on in life to accept the spouse's reactions.

By being open with each other and talking about everything, Bridie and Paul were able to communicate and accept how each other felt through their ordeals. They have taken what they have learned and put it to the best use possible, that of helping others who have suffered through the death of a child. They are well aware of how much the outpouring of love, which continues to this day, has helped them through the worst of times.

Although Bridie and Paul lost their only two children and chose not to add any others to their lives, they both believe things happen for a reason and though we may not know immediately what those reasons are, acceptance and a new perspective helped them to move on with their lives. For Bridie it is through a program to help professionals understand the grieving process which in turn helps the grieving parents. She didn't want to end up an angry, bitter person. She knows her kids wouldn't have wanted that. She says it is for them she does all this, not only for herself. Paul is content in knowing that he survived one of the worst outcomes of such a tragic loss, that of overcoming all the anger and rage he felt at life in general. People were there to listen to his cry for help, and Paul will never forget the outpouring of true compassion and friendship offered by those who cared.

Bridie gave me a poem she wrote that I'd like to share with you. It was written four years after Paul Jr. died. The depth of the pain even four years later is very evident.

Words?
How can mere words
    adequately express what is in my heart?

How can mere words
    describe the pain and anguish?

How can mere words
    convey, so some other being will understand,
    to the depths of my soul, the pain I feel?

I picture myself being held…
    by God
    close, with His arms securely around me,
    holding me close and
    me just sobbing.
    Sobbing all the pain and hurt.

No words
Words can't begin to tell it.
    Only the tension in my body
    trying not to let it all out at once.

Fearful it will be too overwhelming
    but not able to hold it in any longer.

Needing to just be held…
    by God.

20

Aaron

"I had a difficult time rebuilding my life without my son...learning to live without him and with how he died is still the greatest challenge of my life...I sent him to his death unknowingly, out of concern, love and with the best of intentions...I know I am not responsible for his death...but meshing my intellect with my heart is very difficult."

Sally

Guilt can tear you apart. To this day I live with the knowledge that I probably sent a reluctant Aaron to his death when he went to the wilderness camp. But when I think of Aaron now, I concentrate on the knowledge that I was blessed to have him in my life. No matter what anyone else says or thinks, I know that my life has been touched by an angel. He taught me more in his 16 years than I ever taught him. Aaron died in 1994 at a wilderness therapy camp in Utah of peritonitis from a perforated ulcer.

Aaron was different from all the other children; an old soul. He seemed to understand things that most children his age did not. He was passionate about his fellow man. He couldn't understand prejudice, war, unkindness. It broke his heart to see the homeless. He couldn't tolerate unfairness of any kind. This world was a difficult place for Aaron.

In third grade a friend of his was being picked on. He called the friend's mother and explained to her that her son would need "extra love and understanding" when he got home because of what was going on at school. This little boy's mom shared this story at Aaron's funeral. Another story that brings a smile to me is when Aaron befriended the homeless in our neighborhood by putting peanut butter and jelly sandwiches in an old milk slot of our home for them to eat. I tried to explain that could be dangerous, but all he knew is that they were hungry, had no home and no one to take care of them. He thought it only right that we share with them because we had plenty to eat. He understood at a very young age that we are our brother's keeper, and no one could tell him any differently. He even explained to me once how he talked to friends who have died and to Jesus. "But they don't talk back," I said. He grabbed my hand, put it on his chest, smiled and said, "Mommy, you don't hear them with your ears; you hear them with your heart."

When I was with Aaron, I always knew that I was in the presence of someone special. I truly believed that God put him in my life to bring me spirituality. And he did indeed.

As Aaron got older he began to write as an outlet for his frustration and confusion. He was articulate and had a command of the English language. His poetry was insightful beyond his years. Aaron expected a lot from himself and others. It made it very hard for him to be a child. When he made a mistake, he had a hard time forgiving himself. If he did something wrong, he felt that he was a "bad" person because he should have known better. Growing up was hard on him.

Aaron was respected and admired by both students and teachers. He was compassionate, funny, provocative and challenging. He had integrity and stood up for what he believed. He was involved environmentally and politically, was a leader in school and had well thought out opinions. Instead of buying Christmas presents, he would donate to the AIDS Foundation in memory of some friend. Parents I knew envied our relationship. We were very connected.

Aaron's struggles began his freshman year of high school. He started smoking pot, did some LSD and questioned our values, society's values and his own. Things at home became strained. Before the drugs we had always been each other's best friend. I was his confidant. In retrospect we were probably too close. He began to make terrible decisions, withdraw, lose his way. Our home became a battlefield. Something was terribly wrong, and I had to help him. We took him out of school.

I had heard about a wilderness therapy program from a friend. It seemed like a dream come true. It was for troubled teens who were struggling with growing up. The program promised positive results. They guaranteed they would build self-esteem through hiking, teaching survival skills and meeting with a therapist. The kids would hike all day in the Utah desert, set up camp at night and sit around the campfire and discuss their issues. The idea of being out in the wilderness, away from the distractions of music and friends, with God and nature, almost sounded like a vacation. Part of the program was having to write in a journal each night, and writing was Aaron's life. Never once did the program indicate that it was any kind of boot camp. We would have never put Aaron in that type of environment. After meeting with the owners, asking all the appropriate questions, we decided to enroll Aaron for the 63 days.

Aaron died on the 30th day from a perforated ulcer. But in reality Aaron died because he was denied medical attention, starved and suffered from hypothermia. Because he was denied food 14 of the 20 days he hiked, his stomach began to eat away at itself causing the ulcer to perforate. Never once did the camp make us aware that anything was wrong.

Aaron wasn't allowed to write for the first three weeks. I wrote him one letter and called the camp several times a week to check on his progress. I didn't know he was sick.

Criminal charges were brought against the owners and six of the employees. Most of them plea-bargained to negligent homicide and received community service, a fine and probation. One counselor was found guilty and sentenced to one year in jail, but served only two months.Through the trial we found out that Aaron had lost control of his bodily functions 10 days before he died. When he asked to see a doctor because he was in pain, no one believed him. Additional treatment of him on the hikes was horrible. He was too sick to carry his pack, so to punish him they took away his food and blankets. He was made to sleep on the ground in 28-degree weather. I honestly didn't think I could ever survive sitting through the trial and learning all the terrible things that were done to my son.

Aaron's story attracted nationwide attention. CNN, Dateline and Leeza did several stories.

The horror we experienced when we saw his body was inconceivable. He was emaciated, looked like a skeleton and had lost 30 pounds. There were bruises all over his frail body and open sores on his feet. My husband collapsed when he saw him. I don't think we would have believed that it was our son if it weren't for the childhood scar above his right eye. I will never be able to get that vision of my son out of my mind. It was a nightmare that I would never wake up from.

When the trial and media coverage ended, it was as if Aaron died all over again. All the newspapers had kept him alive for me. Now he was yesterday's news. I was devastated all over again. When the trial ended, our struggle as a family really began. We had to learn to live without him. Our other son, Jarid, was lost without his brother. In a way he lost his parents too, because we were not the same people we were before Aaron died. Grief is a terribly lonely emotion. It is impossible to help anyone else when you are so consumed with grief yourself. It can tear families apart. We were blessed that Aaron's death eventually brought us even closer.

I had a difficult time rebuilding my life without Aaron. Learning to live without him and with how he died is still the greatest challenge of my life. I am his mother, and I sent him off to his death. Unknowingly, of course. I sent him out of concern, love and with the best of intentions, but it still cost him his life. I hardly think naivete is a very good defense. Intellectually, I know that I am not responsible for his death, that it was the camp and its staff. But meshing my intellect with my heart is very difficult. I probably will struggle with this for the rest of my life.

Healing is a strange thing. It happens slowly, over time if you let it. What really seemed to save my life was beading. After Aaron died I began beading necklaces and rosaries. I spent hours creating these objects of beauty. It kept me focused. The rosaries in particular brought me a lot of peace. I felt somehow that they were truly connected to Aaron. I believe that every time someone prays with a rosary I've made and sold, Aaron feels my energy. Each prayer is like kisses and hugs for him.

I was commissioned to make a rosary for the Pope, which was quite an honor. When the rosary was given to him, he also was given an article written in the LA Times about my son's death. Weeks later I received a letter from his Holiness, written through the monsignor, expressing his sorrow and saying that he would be praying for Aaron. He also said that he hoped that my husband and I would find peace. I was stunned, but reminded that miracles do happen everyday. We just need to be willing to recognize them when they do.

My jewelry is now sold through a gallery where we live. I am also taking creative writing at a local college and hope to someday write a book.

My husband, Bob, is a strong, intellectual, steady guy. He has always been my rock. But Aaron's death almost destroyed him. I honestly didn't think he would survive. Bob and Aaron were really beginning to connect. Aaron was very much like his dad. Bob's work is his passion, and he spent most of his time working when the boys were younger. He never got the chance to spend the kind of time with Aaron that he wanted. He mourned all the time that he missed with him. I mourned having spent maybe too much time with him, not giving him his space. As I look back, I had a hard time letting him grow up. Bob has survived, and I believe is at peace with Aaron's death. He is a very spiritual man, attends church regularly and truly believes that Aaron is in a better place.

I, too, am spiritual, although I do not find solace in church. I do believe that there is life after death and that my son is in a much better place. But, I can't say that it brings me much peace. I want him right here with me. I know that is selfishness, a human quality I can't seem to overcome.

The one thing that was so hard for me was that I never got to say goodbye to Aaron, to hold him in my arms and tell him how sorry I was. Since his death, I have had some absolutely life altering experiences. I know without a doubt that there is life on the other side and that our loved ones are closer than we realize. I had the incredible gift of hearing from Aaron after he died. There is a well-known psychic medium named George Anderson. I attended a seminar where he and Dr. Raymond Moody were speaking. Dr. Moody is a world-renowned authority on near death experiences and Mr. Anderson communicates with spirits on the other side. When he began to speak, he explained that he was a conduit from which the spirits speak. Not everyone would hear from a loved one, and there is no control over who comes through. He said whoever comes through is who you need to hear from. He said, "There is one spirit who has been busting my chops ever since he heard I was coming here. Does anyone here take the name Aaron?" He proceeded to tell me things that only my son would know, very personal and private messages to both Bob and I. Aaron did say that he forgives me and that he knows that I didn't know what was going on.

That was just the beginning of some magical conversations with Aaron. I believe in my heart that I was given these experiences by the grace of God. There are days that I still cry myself to sleep. I still struggle, but considering the circumstances of how he died, I think I do very well.

I have tried to behave in a way that Aaron would be proud. I have tried to handle his death and the trial with as much dignity as I can. We have two choices when a child dies. We can take our own life, or we can live. You go on somehow, you just do. Life is a gift, and I chose to live, not with one foot in the grave, not bitter and full of hate, but trying to live life to the fullest. I have a husband and son who need me. I need them. We are still a family and Aaron would want us to pull together and not mourn for him but celebrate his life. That is what we try to do.

On Aaron's birthday each year at 6:56 p.m., the moment he was born, we send colorful helium balloons in the air. His friends still come, even though we don't send invitations. We all gather together and read his poetry and give thanks that he was in our lives.

Observations of Sally

Sally made it through what one can only describe as a journey through hell. She tried so hard to help the son she loved so much, yet the end results were only disaster and continual guilt. Sally realized that if she let it, the guilt could consume her. Aaron asked for help; he also asked not to be sent to the camp. She says she made a bad judgment sending him there, but at that moment it was the best decision she was capable of making. Is she responsible for his death? Not really. She knows that, but how can you not continually ask yourself that question. It is part of the territory of parenthood. We feel it is our job to keep our child safe; and if they die, it is our fault. The "if onlys" can haunt you. One child psychologist says that no mother can be attuned to her child 100 percent of the time. We do our best and that is all we can do. Sally's intentions were good. She wanted her son to get help. She saw this as the best solution available to her.

As it turned out, Sally's role in this horror story was small. Other factors were largely responsible. Talking with others who truly understand what you're going through can help a person look at their guilt realistically. Sally understands that feeling less guilty won't take away the anger, pain or sadness, but surely it is worth the effort to take a realistic look at forgiving yourself.

Sally is a strong woman who wants to live for the rest of her family who loves her, so each day she wakes up, gets out of bed, whether she wants to or not, and continues to be productive. She is obviously looking towards future goals when she mentions going back to school and learning how to write. She sees a book in her future. She doesn't know exactly what the book will be about, but chances are that Aaron will be a part of it.

21

Peggy

"I am part of a type of self-realization, self-improvement group…where you truly learn to understand yourself and realize the power of the subconscious mind…The group helped a lot, as did the Chinese philosophy that says when there is bad, there is an equal amount of good. You just have to look for it. Even though a death is devastating, if you look hard, you can find some good as a result of it…"

Floyd

With a gift of clairvoyance, I knew instantly when I received a phone call late one night from my ex-wife saying one of our daughters had been in a car accident, that my daughter would not survive her injuries.

In 1970 Peggy, 17-years-old, had gone to pick up her graduation pictures in San Jose, California, had dinner in Los Gatos and was coming over to give me one of her pictures. I never found out specifically what happened, but I know that the driver lost control of the car near an off ramp before an overpass. The car flipped, and ended up hitting a concrete abutment supporting the overpass. The driver fell out. Peggy had her seat belt on and remained in the car. When they found her she was severely injured and taken to a hospital. The phone call told me she was stable, and if she lasted the night, would be okay. I knew in my heart she was not going to make it and told my second wife that before leaving for the hospital with her. In the emergency room where everyone in the family had gathered, I heard a code blue alert and knew it was for her. She died three hours after arriving at the hospital.

I have a family history of clairvoyance. My grandfather was very perceptive, and I inherited a little of it. Peggy's death was not the first time I'd had that experience. Long before, I'd gone to visit my grandparents before moving to start a new job. In church that Sunday my grandfather started singing some of the songs, something he didn't do very often, and suddenly I knew he was saying to me it was the last time I would ever see him. We looked at each other later on when it was time to say good-bye, and I realized he knew the same thing. Three weeks later he was killed in a blacksmith shop accident. A wheel on the grinder broke loose and hit him in the chest.

I've also had several instances where I do things that are kind of strange. The subconscious mind, I believe, has your complete program, like a computer, of what your life is supposed to be like and, like a computer, you can reprogram it if you choose to do that, but if you don't, it will play out the program that is there. One time I was driving and suddenly put my foot on the brake at a blind intersection where I had the right of way, instead of accelerating through. My wife said, "Why are you braking?" At that moment a car ran the stop sign. I would have hit it if I hadn't had my foot on the brake.

After the accident, I couldn't find a necklace I'd given Peggy and thought it may have been lost on the freeway. I walked the freeway to find it. Police stopped me, and I explained what we were doing. No, we didn't find it there, but it did turn up later on in some of her things. At the hospital they gave me her clothes. I had the hardest time throwing them away. It was as though as long as I had her clothes I was still holding onto a part of her. There's a lot to whoever said a parent shouldn't have to suffer the death of a child, that everyone should go in his time and the parent should be allowed to go first.

Except for my daughter's death, I have worked through most of my major occurrences and decisions in life such as job changes, divorce and personal problems. I meditate on them and ask my subconscious or God or whoever you want to relate to, for resolutions. I read books on self-help. As for my marriage to Peggy's mother, I resolved in my mind that she wasn't going to do anything to continue the marriage and then I ended it. On job interviews I always did role playing as I did in my personal life. On any kind of stress related occasion, if I knew it was coming up, I went through training, role-playing the situation several different ways. When I actually got into the situation, I generally had covered anything that would come up so it wasn't a surprise to me.

My second wife and I were part of a type of a self-realization, self-improvement group that started in the Stanford, California, area. In this group you truly learn to understand yourself and realize the power of the subconscious mind. It was called "Challenge To Change" or "Build the Earth." There were several groups in the area that operated with the same people, some with slightly different names, all with the same purpose.

The group was originally started by a professor of law at Stanford University and his wife and nine other couples. We had individual family groups with leaders, seminars and retreats in the Santa Cruz Mountains. It was based on the teachings of Jesus, even though it was not denomination oriented or strictly religious oriented. You were challenged. Was this your true feeling or was this something coming from you mentally? There was no physical activity except hugging people occasionally and free falling in a circle to develop trust. They worked on marriage relationships, personal relationships, and your relationship with a higher being, the spiritual world.

When I first started in the group I wouldn't cry at anything. I'd been taught and conditioned not to show emotions. When I did something wrong, my dad would spank me until I cried and then spank me until I stopped crying. I became very controlled to the point I didn't recognize I had emotions when I started in this group. We were in it for close to five years and were conference leaders for a while. We had been in the group three years when Peggy was killed. The group helped a lot; that together with my personal experiences with my grandfather.

At this time I also read books on the subconscious mind, self-improvement, clairvoyance, death and beyond and out of body experiences. I took a couple of courses at Santa Clara University on past lives and improving your E.S.P. I spent an evening with a high school teacher, who was in the group, discussing how he could do out of body travel.

One thing we were told by our group was that no matter what happens, even though you may feel it's bad, as in Chinese philosophy, there is always good, too. You have the yin and the yang, the Chinese symbol, showing that when there is bad, there is an equal amount of good. You just have to look for it. Even though a death is devastating, if you look hard, you can find some good as a result of it.

The good from Peggy's death is that during the funeral arrangements my ex-wife and I were having some difficulty. My ex-wife wanted Peggy cremated, and I didn't. My current wife intervened. My ex-wife hated my new wife and made it very clear. During the visitation she came up to my wife and said, "I don't hate you anymore." And after that they had a reasonably good relationship. The anger was no longer there. It's a shame that something like that has to happen for some good to come of it. It should have been able to happen without Peggy's death, but that turned out to be the stimulus.

Peggy was my favorite child. This doesn't mean I didn't love the other four children from my first marriage or the two from my second marriage, but she was special. The best part of her was her empathy and consideration for others. At eight Peggy had made pictures of angels and other representations of Christmas and brought it to my new wife as a gift. There was no resentment toward her from Peggy as there was with the other children. Peggy wanted to come stay with us for a while, but after talking to her mother she came back and said she couldn't leave her mother, that her mother depended on her too much. She continued to visit and babysit for us, even when the others stopped coming to visit.

I don't do any special remembrances for Peggy, but I am reminded of her by my granddaughter born in December 1970, six weeks after Peggy's death. Her name is Peggy, named for her aunt. My Peggy's ashes are in an urn in a niche in a San Jose cemetery. I only visited once. Visiting that niche is not visiting her. She's gone. Her spirit is gone. I can visit the spirit just as well sitting in this room as I can going to the cemetery to visit a niche in a wall.

I remember at the hospital when my mother died. When I went to leave, the nurse said, "Don't you want to spend some time here with her?" I said, "No, she's not here anymore, anymore than you would like to visit an empty house that had been your home after everyone had moved out." She looked at me like I was weird.

A fellow who worked for me called when his son had died in an auto accident in 1991. He called me because he knew I'd gone through it, and asked if I had any advice for him, asked if I ever got over my daughter's death. "No," I told him, "you never get over it."

Observations of Floyd

Floyd calls himself strange sometimes because of his clairvoyance, his ability to know what will happen and incidents that support these happenings make him feel different. It doesn't bother him what others think. He is now married to Rose, a decendant of the Hungarian gypsies, who is a palm reader and a psychic. They both openly discuss their gifts with people who are interested.

Many books and psychologists have reiterated the great power of the subconscious mind. I believe it. You may see it in yourself. I know I have had similar experiences where I think something will happen and then it does. As an example, I seem to know when the phone will ring during the day a few seconds before it does and usually know who will be on the other end. I don't see Floyd as unusual at all. I see him as a man who has a gift to be able to find good out of devastation and to realize it is important to continue to look in that direction.

After 30 years it was still difficult for Floyd to talk about Peggy. Sometimes, he told me, "I'll just be sitting on the couch and she'll just come to mind, as I remember with pride the good person she was." When he spoke about knowing in his heart she was not going to survive the accident, he had to pause to catch his breath. At other times during the conversation he was silent as tears came to his eyes and for a moment he could not speak. I think it surprised him how overwhelmed he became and how strongly it still affects him. After such a long period of time, we assume parents can talk freely and without too much emotion about their dead children. But that is not always the case, nor should they ever be embarrassed about any display of emotions. "As you can see," he said, "I've never gotten over it." And why should he? Our children are never forgotten.

Floyd spends his retirement doing woodworking, preparing tax returns at the small business he owns, and doing volunteer tax work for low income and elderly once a week.

22

Jennifer

"We realized how important our relationship was as a couple…we were drawn to each other for support…we prayed together a lot…we found meaningful things in readings that were hopeful, encouraging and spiritual…we felt sustained by our faith and by our love for each other…"

Beverly and Wayne

God has taught us tremendous lessons as a couple. When our daughter, Jennifer, 25-years-old, died in 1983, Beverly and I had just been through three years of caring for her and being sustained by our faith and by our love for each other…Wayne

Jennifer was, as Wayne called her, a velvet covered brick, very strong but a very soft heart. She met her husband at a Christian college where he was finishing seminary training. She was an excellent seamstress who wanted to go into design. She was accepted in a home economics program at the University of Minnesota but changed her major to elementary education to stay near her fiancee.They were married two years when she became ill. She had incredible strength through all of this. She trusted God that if this is what he ordained for her life, she would submit to that plan. The support was tremendous, from friends, neighbors, the church that Wayne was Pastor of and the people at the college Jennifer and her husband attended and graduated from, to the entire town of Deerfield, Illinois, where we all lived at the time. With all this and the love of her family, Jennifer was able to cope with this illness...Beverly

Just before Jennifer graduated she had a grand mal seizure. She was tested and the results were negative. For a year she took medicine to control the seizures, but she began to feel worse as time went on and was examined again. The doctors found a rapidly growing tumor. As much as possible was removed in three subsequent surgeries. She lived for three years with the illness, but Beverly and I tried, as a family, to make it the best three years we could...Wayne

Jennifer received occasional suggestions to go to different healers, but she said no. "The medical world and everyone are doing what they can for me," she would say to them. "I don't have to grasp after straws." Wayne and I wanted to do anything possible and did but felt ultimately she was in God's hands. Most importantly, we wanted her days to be good days surrounded by friends and family...Beverly

During those three years I just dealt with my grief. I couldn't fathom life without my daughter. There was a heaviness in my chest, and I cried so hard in the shower each morning, I wondered if people could die from grief. It was so all consuming for me. I wasn't angry at God. I wasn't bitter. I just dealt with the fact that I didn't want to lose this precious daughter. I didn't know if I could look forward to life if God took her. I would get on my knees and cry out to God that if he didn't help me I couldn't bear the grief. Then I would let the water from the shower wash away my tears so that I could take care of my family: Wayne, Jennifer and my other daughter who was eight years younger, Stephanie. I knew I wanted to make the most of these days I had with Jennifer...Beverly

My wife and I realized how important our relationship was as a couple. A lot of couples retreat into their own world, one works a lot to dull the pain, the other one moves in a different direction. Instead of bonding, they find themselves separating and after several years they don't even know each other. Beverly and I were drawn to each other for support. We prayed together a lot. We shared scriptures. We found meaningful things in readings that were hopeful, encouraging and spiritual. We shared thoughts with Jennifer that were meaningful not only about this life, but eternal life, what God says about our relationship with Him. Jennifer, in turn, also shared with us…Wayne

Stephanie was in a boarding school in North Carolina when Jennifer became ill. She couldn't have led a normal life if she'd been at home with Jennifer around, and I wouldn't have left Stephanie alone to spend time with Jennifer. But since she was away, I was able to spend more time with Jenny. It was a gift to have those days with her, and I'll always treasure them…Beverly

It is horrible to lose a child. I can't think of anything worse. Bev and I felt sustained by our faith and by our love for each other. Family was important. During those three years we had a lot of family experiences together that were good. Jennifer had a lot of friends in her life. They would visit often, and our home was a joyful place filled with singing, good food and fellowship, so that even though it was the hardest, most painful time of our life, it was also a time when we enjoyed each other…Wayne

During the last two years, Jennifer and her husband lived with Wayne and I a lot of the time, and all five of us bonded together. Often all of us could be found in our big bed at night watching television. The unity we had as a family was a real source of strength. I wanted Jennifer to feel surrounded not only by God's love but also by our love too. We were never given any hope. Realistically, we knew her days were numbered. But most of the time until the last few months she was feeling good. My prayer was that our home would be a happy, joyful place, open to all her friends and ours. She was a people person and that was obvious in everything she did and the people who were always in our home...Beverly

As a father I could see Stephanie was going through a lot of pain. They were best friends, very connected and had an unusual bond. It was hard for Stephanie, while being a young teenager, to see her sister go through so much suffering. It was also hard to be the only child left...Wayne

When Jennifer was in the hospital, the room was full of flowers, family and friends. Wayne and I tried to make each day special. The Chaplain at the hospital thought we were in massive denial, that what we were experiencing was a cover-up of our grief. I told him I was crying my heart out at home and that what he was seeing here was a personal relationship we had with God, that we have asked Him to intervene and give us strength to get through each day. We were not, I told him, experiencing denial...Beverly

When Jennifer died, I felt I had grieved so much in those three years, now I was just lonesome for her. I had already done my grieving. I was also thankful Wayne was in the ministry. In a sense I was forced into forgetting how I felt. People were hurting and they needed the pastor's wife. Two weeks after Jennifer's death I had to go to a hospital to visit someone and then to a funeral. I told myself I couldn't do it. But I knew I needed to be there, so I went. At the one year anniversary I was forced to be with people at a single's retreat and was grateful to God that I wasn't going to have time to cry that weekend. I said, "Thank you, God, for forcing me to get beyond myself." I missed Jennifer so much, I understood anyone who became a hermit and stayed stuck for the rest of their lives. At this retreat I met a girl in her 20's whose mom died of cancer, and she asked if she could be a daughter to us and I could be a mom to her. We would have missed out on that blessing. She has been a delight to us over the years...Beverly

I don't know how anyone can go through this without faith. I couldn't have made it. I would have been a different person. It brought faith into more of a reality at that time because what Beverly and I believed was very sustaining…Wayne

After 17 years, on rare occasions, I still cry at home. Tears release a lot of emotions; they are good for you. People don't realize this. Sometimes a song will trigger tears, and one time I broke down when visiting a friend at the hospital. When I walked in, I began reliving all the hospital visits Wayne and I made to see Jennifer. It took me by surprise; I didn't realize it would affect me so…Beverly

It is very hard for me to go to the cemetery when we are back in Minneapolis where she is buried, so I don't go, nor does Wayne. Another thing that is hard for me is that I have yet to reread all the letters she sent me when she and her husband traveled. I have them all, and one day I hope to be able to read them, but not yet. I wear some of her jewelry and keep some of the items she created as a seamstress. I've tried to avoid anything that would add to the sorrow I carry in my heart…Beverly

There were a few things that kept me going and were very important to me after Jennifer's death. One was the great relationship Wayne and I had with her husband. He truly was, and is, a son to us. The friendships I had and still do were also important. Friends made me go shopping, to plays, to lunch so we could laugh together and minister to each other if they, too, were going through bad times. It is too overpowering to pull into yourself when grieving, and you become lonely. Grief shared is very powerful. My friends were very supportive. Also being in the bible sustained me. Everyday I opened it and would say, "Give me strength to get through today." God got me through…Beverly

I will never be the same person I was before Jennifer's death and neither will Wayne. We see life entirely different now. We don't take things for granted. We value and treasure what we have. You learn to be kind and gentle with people when you realize the kind of pain that can dwell within our hearts and not be observable on the outside. It gives me a great empathy for people who are hurting. It takes away your judgmental attitudes because you have no comprehension of the grief that can be inside a person...Beverly

Beverly and I do a lot of counseling at the ministry, but also a lot of teaching. We teach marriage classes, lead home studies classes on how to build a strong marriage, teach marriage intimacy classes and also do bible study. We've gone to mission fields to encourage missionaries as singles and couples; we've held a marriage conference and have even met with pastors in our own congregation to see how their own marriages are going since they minister so much to others. We have been through leadership training seminars, but much of our training is on the job training and being involved in peoples' lives. All this has made us look at our own relationship, and this experience drew us together even more, making us stronger...Wayne

The greatest joy for Wayne and I during these past 17 years, along with our faith, is our young daughter Stephanie and her family. They are a daily blessing to us.—Beverly

I am able to challenge a lot of moms: "Don't take your kids for granted," I say. "Invest in your kids right now, enjoy every minute and don't count on having them around tomorrow."...Beverly

My wife and I will continue to enjoy the memory of Jennifer. She is always in our hearts. We think of her all the time. All the memories are good ones. We were so close. We've always had a great relationship with our daughters. We did everything together it was possible to do. We live with no regrets. There was nothing more we could have done with our girls that we didn't do. That has given us peace...Wayne

Observations of Beverly and Wayne

Beverly and Wayne have always had a closely knit family, which in turn gave them the strength to endure the death of their oldest daughter. As I spoke to these two, I felt they were the type of people you would go to for

advice, for support and for love. It was obvious they both care so much for others, for their feelings, for their joys and for their pain. To be able to go through this together as they did and survive not only intact, but also to come out of it even stronger is a real feat and takes much courage.

Beverly and Wayne are thankful they have so much to remember from Jennifer's last three years, lots of happy memorable events they can always treasure because of the wonderful relationship they were able to have with both of their daughters.

Beverly wonders how parents survive who do not get to say good-bye to their children, because of a sudden death. She finds the idea incomprehensible and even asked me about the feelings I went through. She wanted to know how to help these people that she may come in contact with or minister to at her own church. She knows, because of her grief, that there is lots of pain inside a person that others can't see, and she wants to understand that pain. So does Wayne. By listening and counseling others, they hope to gain that knowledge.

Faith can be very powerful. Without their faith, Beverly and Wayne say they don't know what they would have done. When you know your child is dying, you try to make the rest of their life as happy and as comfortable as possible, even though you are not sure you will have the strength to go on each day. This couple believes God gave them that strength and say they will always trust in Him. Wherever He may lead them, Beverly and Wayne know there will be a reason and a purpose.

23

John

"My son gave me such strength with everything he went through. I knew that if he, through all his pain, could keep his witty sense of humor in tact…I could do this too."

Marion

There are no guarantees in this life. From all the reading I've done about people who have lived through bad times, it showed me I wasn't alone. No matter who you are or how much money you have, things happen. For me, the death of my son, John, from AIDS complications has been the most shattering experience of my life. I move on each day. I get up, do what I have to do and at the end of each day, I still have the feeling something's missing, because it is. It's tough, but I do one day at a time. I know I must go on. John would want me to.

John Anthony (Johnny, as he was affectionately called by close friends and family) died in 1995, at age 27, from AIDS. When he was diagnosed in late 1988, he told me immediately. I knew he was gay. It did not matter to me. He was still the same loving and giving son he had always been. We were extremely close as I was a single mother for most of his life. I felt we were connected at the hip; we did everything together. He was my best friend and confidant and would have made my old age more humorous and easier to deal with, that's for sure.

His father and I were divorced when John was 3-years-old, but he remained close to his dad. It was tough on his dad too. His dad and I spent lots of time together with John at the hospital and at home during the last three months of his life.

For six and a half years John was on medicines that seemed to work for him. Then suddenly his body stopped responding to them and he would break out in a rash. His last year he was in and out of the hospital. We were able to take one final trip together to St. Thomas in 1994. He was hospitalized in late September. By mid-November there was nothing else that could be done for him. I brought him home to die.

Even though I had lived for six years knowing how ill he was, I was still in shock and disbelief when it happened. If he can survive until he is 40, I told myself, he will have lived a decent number of years. I never expected it to be so fast. Six and a half years was not considered a long time, particularly since they had medicines that were prolonging life to a greater extent than ever before. But it was not to be.

John was a trooper through it all. His greatest asset was his sense of humor up to the very end. For his friends who I still keep in contact with, it is one of the best things they remember about him. He could snap you out of a bad day. He always had a good attitude. Most of all, he held 'me' up. He would ask me not to allow visitors sometimes, so it could just be the two of us. We had our best talks in the middle of the night, at 3 or 4 a.m.

In the last few years, John went back to college, did well and studied hard. He received a B.A. in Psychology, but never got to use his skills. When he graduated in 1993, he was already too sick. He also enrolled in a nursing class, but never got to finish it. That made him feel bad, but he had to give it up; he had no choice.

Before John died, I got into counseling to help me get through it. I learned to deal with each day and try to make the best of the time we had together. The uncertainty of not knowing whether the medicines would work was hard to deal with. After he died, I continued counseling for about four years, stopping because my counselor retired, and I didn't want to start over with someone new.

When John died I changed. I became extremely selfish. I take care of me now. I have a don't care kind of attitude in the sense of, what will be, will be. Nothing is important to me anymore. He was my life, and with his death died his dreams and my every reason for being. However, I have from deep within me, found the strength to go on in the best way I can.

I don't have the resources to do the many things I'd like to in his memory, but one of the events that I took part in a few months after his death that helped me along in my grieving and put more closure to what happened was to get involved with the famous AIDS Memorial Quilt Names Project. Some of his friends and I got together and did a quilt panel. We were able to present it at Drew University in New Jersey which had the display at that time. On the picture of the quilt panel are five stars, each has the name of those who took part in its creation: Mom, Fino, Nancy, Stephen and Thomas. The scroll is a quote from Shakespeare's *Romeo and Juliet*, Act 3, Scene 1:

> "*...and when he shall die,*
> *Take him and cut him out in little stars,*
> *And he will make the face of heaven so fine,*
> *That all the world will be in love with night,*
> *And pay no worship to the garish sun.*"

The dates on the panel read 1967-1995.

In October 1996 a few of his friends and I attended the Names Project display of the quilt in Washington, D.C. It stretched from the Capitol to the Washington Monument. One night they did a candlelight march from the Capitol to the Lincoln Memorial. Candles were glowing along the entire procession. It was a breathtaking experience.

The full quilt is housed in San Francisco. When you look at the panels, you can see that it is well cared for. The designs are not frayed or dirty in any way. I have done volunteer work when it was displayed near my home. I answer questions about the quilt, take care of people walking around and see that it does not get soiled. Items such as T-shirts, books, keychains and bumperstickers are also sold where it is displayed to keep the project going. I have recently become a member of the Northern New Jersey Chapter of the AIDS Memorial Quilt as a result of my desire to be part of all this.

Another beautiful event I take part in is an AIDS mass once a month at a local church. When I walk into the church, I sign a book and the names are read at the mass. It validates the child to hear his name spoken like that. It's very healing for me. I haven't talked to anyone there because I believe most of these people are dealing with loved ones who are still living with the disease. I attended one support group for a while, where I did meet one woman I have become good friends with. I tried The Compassionate Friends group but did not feel comfortable there. Since John was my only child I had no one else to talk about. Many TCF members talk about their other children or grandchildren, a comfort level I could not identify with. It was at one TCF meeting I met a woman who gave me the address for the Alive Alone Newsletter.

Through the newsletter I found a group of parents of only children that holds conferences every other year called 'In Loving Memory.' I have attended those and am very open about the fact that my son died from AIDS. I am not afraid to speak about it. There are those with similar stories that won't be that open because of the stigma attached to the disease. At this conference workshops are held throughout the days dealing with issues surrounding children's deaths; there is a banquet and a candle lighting. A video is shown of all the children from pictures we send, along with soothing music. It is very powerful and extremely moving.

In the Alive Alone newsletter which is related to the conference, I read similar stories and get comfort from knowing I'm not alone in what happened. It is a peaceful feeling. I am a great believer in group therapy as is done at these conferences. It works. You get a sense that if other people can survive, you can too.

In New York I have participated in AIDS Walk New York every year since 1994. Celebrity speakers talk in Central Park where the walk starts. We have raised thousands of dollars doing this. In my home state of New Jersey I also particiate in walks.

On my car is a bumper sticker that says "Loved and remembered, John Anthony." A couple from California started making them after their child died. I have a good supply so that when I get a new car, one is waiting to go on it. When I see people look at it, I just smile; it's a great feeling.

Most of my friends and family knew John had AIDS. They were very understanding and helpful. Some were in denial. They were afraid to touch him, afraid they would get the disease, a fallacy still prevalent today. I find I want to be around people who want to talk about my son. Those that don't, I stay away from, particularly those who pretend he never existed.

Counselors tell you it is wise to change your habits after your child dies. One of the things I do now is spend Christmas in Texas with my brother and his family. My sister, niece and I go out to dinner to celebrate John's birthday each year. They live nearby.

On holidays friends want me to come over. Most of the time I don't want to go. It bothers me to try to fit in with other peoples' families. Sometimes I just prefer being alone. I'm better that way. I look at pictures, and I do my own remembering.

One of the objects I enjoy in my home is a special lighted hutch. In it are personal belongings from my son. I have a yearbook, his glasses, his license plate, a hand print from first grade, his graduation certificate, photos and many other things that I can look at whenever I feel like it. In those moments I am close to him.

I now work as a patient account representative for a hospital. I credit my son for the new career. I had a home health aide that came in a couple of hours a day near the end because it was tough for me to care for him 24 hours a day. I considered becoming a health aide, but when I put my resume out there, I was hired to be a coordinator and then transferred to the billing area, where I remain today.

I read a few grief books, but mostly inspirational books about people who have lived through bad times and experienced similar circumstances. It shows you're not alone. No matter who you are or how much money you have, things happen. There are no guarantees in this life. I got a lot of strength from that.

I want others to know they must cherish every moment with their child. In my case this was a longtime commitment that I knew would ultimately end. You want to be there for your child, and I was.

Observations of Marion

Marion was anxious to talk about John because she knows that it is helpful to acknowledge his existence as an important part of her life. When the interview was done she said she had a good feeling and that sometimes just talking is the best therapy.

Marion seems to have found a lot of comfort and part of a greater family as she continues her work to help fight AIDS as best she can, participating in the walks, as a volunteer and creating a panel for the memorial quilt. There are now more than 40,000 quilt panels. Recently, the National Endowment for the Arts gave a $47,000 grant to help individually catalog every panel. Letters, biographies and photos, also submitted with the panels, are going to be placed on an accessible Internet database. In this way global access for everyone will be available, and all the information will be preserved for generations. The quilt has done much to educate millions *about HIV and AIDS. It is an impressive tribute to those who have died from the disease. According to Marion, all you need is a few friends, some fabric and an imagination, and you can create whatever you want in your child's honor. There is also a National High School Quilt Program which has started to go into high schools in every state to educate younger people on the disease and its prevention.*

Worldwide, there are over 30 million cases of AIDS; over 1 million are children under 15. Almost 12 million deaths occur each year, according to a United Nations study. The United States has reported over 650,000 cases and approximately 400,000 deaths since the epidemic started in 1981 says the Center for Disease Control. There are almost 50,000 new cases each year and one in two happens to someone 25 years of age or younger, as in John's case. Marion used the AIDS service organization (ASO), whose primary purpose is as caregiver to people living with the disease. She felt she could not have done it alone. This group is similar to a Hospice organization.

Many advances in research have recently provided improvements in drug therapy which, in turn, have prolonged life. Deaths from the disease are beginning to drop slightly. The fact that many people can not tolerate the drugs or side effects like John, and the cost being prohibitive, have put a damper on the treatment. There is no cure yet, but we are getting closer. As Marion says, "Until a vaccine is found to prevent or cure the disease, there will always be HIV, but more people will be able to survive for a long time with new medications and have a better quality of life."

24

Robert

"In my second year of grieving I began to do things for the newly bereaved. These were the people behind me, fresh in crisis. When I focused on them, I didn't dwell on my own problems. Soon I noticed that I was in a better place than they were. It was a good measure of my own recovery."

Bernie

I tried so hard to save my son. I kept diving into the helicopter, submerged in the icy water. I didn't stop until a police rescue helicopter arrived about forty minutes later. By then it was hopeless. My son, Robert, 13 years old, drowned after a sightseeing helicopter crashed into the East River in New York City in February, 1990. Of the four passengers and pilot aboard, he was the only one to die. He was tangled up in a way I could not determine, and because of the murky 37 degree water and the darkness inside the inverted, submerged, helicopter, it was impossible to see what the problem was.

I had been trained in emergency techniques during my own pilot training. I knew not to panic, to think quickly and clearly despite the horror, danger and pandemonium around me. But I needed help. The two passengers, both in their twenties, refused my repeated requests for assistance even though they knew a child was trapped in the wreckage. The pilot tried to help briefly, but then swam away. The 24-year-old pilot was never held accountable. He just walked away.

Robert, my only child, was a gentle soul, bright and sensitive. Weighing just over two pounds at birth, he was in excellent health from the moment of his arrival. We brought him home after two months in the just formed neonatal unit. Following my divorce from his mother three years later, Robbie lived with me most weekends, many holidays and for half of each summer.

I was severely depressed after Robbie died. I stopped communicating and stopped eating entirely. Within a month of the crash I had lost 25 pounds. It had been my idea to go on the flight that day. Robbie was in my care, and I could not save his life. These thoughts kept replaying in my head.

My depression completely disabled me for two years. By then, my business was gone. I had remarried two years before the accident and my wife, Rhoda, stuck by my side. She never gave up on me. For five years I continued to see a psychiatrist and used a variety of antidepressants. Between the treatment, the medication and the passing of time, the intensity of the pain lessened and the debilitating moments became fewer and more manageable.

Between stress, submersion and head trauma, portions of my memory have disappeared. Loss of long term memory has caused years of my life to be blank. My short term memory ability was poor from the moment I was pulled out of the water. Short term memory is often a problem as we age, but for me it is an endless parade of people saying, "Hello Bernie," and me not remembering their names or wondering who they are and how they know me.

When I realized I would survive this devastation, I sought out and became involved with a few organizations that help bereaved parents. During my second year of bereavement and against my will, Rhoda volunteered me for The Compassionate Friends hotline. I was asked to talk to newly bereaved parents for a three week period and did it for three months. When you deal with everyone else's problems, you discover you have no time for your own. On the hotline I would also talk to police, hospitals, caregivers, district attorneys. Everyone seemed to call. It got me focused on other people. After three months I was in a different place.

I was also involved with Parents of Murdered Children, a different group entirely from TCF. While TCF focuses mainly on grief, this group focused on anger. Here you are dealing with a justice system that is often not responsive to the death of children. The district attorneys and others dealing with the bereaved parents are excellent and very sensitive to the situation. But the machinery of the justice system often ignores the victim and the parents. Children are brutally murdered, sometimes they are never seen again; other times the killer lives across the street or is out free. In a trial you listen to them blame the child, even if the child is 8-years-old. I received enormous help from the members of the Long Island, New York, chapter.

In the second year I started to do things for others who were really in crisis and when I focused on them, it made me see I was in a better place than they were. I could gauge my recovery on them. I would highly recommend—not at the beginning—but a little bit down the road, starting to focus on helping those who have come behind you.

One newsletter for parents who have lost their only child or all their children is called Alive Alone. Kay Bevington is its founder and guardian. Anyone can subscribe to the newsletter. There is no charge, but donations help offset costs.

In Loving Memory (ILM) is an independent organization that dovetails with Alive Alone. ILM holds a national convention every two years for parents who have lost an only child or all of their children. It was founded and is run by Linda and Glen Neilson. I have attended every conference since ILM started in 1993 and recommend it highly. There is no talk about other children and grandchildren because everyone there has lost all their children. I have been a speaker at several of these conventions talking on "Death and the Justice System from a Parent's Perspective" and "Sudden Death" which is an entirely different path you go through than if you know your child is, for instance, dying of cancer. Since I am planning to practice elder law, I hope to speak at the next convention on "Aging Without Your Child." I believe there are real problems here. No one may be there to look after you when you get old, and there may be physical and financial concerns.

I went to other groups, but got nothing out of them. For people in an area where there is no group, put an ad in the paper saying something like "Bereaved parent seeks others." The phone will start ringing. At my first TCF meeting I thought I might find three or four people attending and was astounded when I walked in and there were 50 people. It made me realize there are a lot of people out there who are in the same situation.

I don't consider myself completely better. I don't think any parent does. I still have some pretty down times when going on seems meaningless. But a lot of things that bothered me earlier in my life seem unimportant now. You have to put it all in perspective. Life and death are important. Whether your furniture comes on time or you're late for a function is not.

One of the things that doesn't faze me anymore is when people say some dumb things to you when your child dies. For example, one acquaintance said, "I know how you feel. My dog died." I don't even get upset at these people because I remember meeting grieving parents before Robert died, and I don't remember saying a single intelligent thing to them. I look back at how insensitive and out of tune I was to what these people were going through. And then it happened to me, and it all became so clear.

Half of my family and friends vanished after Robert died. That is typical. I never heard from them again. Others rose to the occasion, were there from Day 1 and are still there. I didn't expect family to react that way, nor was I very nice when some called five years later. "You weren't there when it was raining. I don't need you when the sun is shining," I told them.

In our home we have pictures on the wall, and we light memorial candles. For a while I went to the cemetery regularly, but now live too far away. We did try on his birthday the first year of his death to have a party. We invited friends who knew him and figured they could tell stories about Robert, but it didn't work. People looked at old pictures and talked about themselves. Robbie was an aside. We never held a party like that again.

Robbie is mentioned at special occasions and at Thanksgiving dinner. I discuss him, but most don't want to hear about him or discuss him at any length. If friends are at my house, they don't have a choice. We don't want him to be forgotten, so we talk about the good memories.

Three years after his death what I did that was very rewarding to me was to set up scholarships and fund projects in the middle school he attended. The school had dedicated a yearbook to him and put up a memorial plaque on the stage. They were very sensitive as to what had happened, and I appreciated it.

One of the projects I funded at his school was to set up a library with books dealing with crisis like the death of a parent, divorce, death of a child, books that would be suitable to kids, teachers, administrators and parents. This way they could see how others dealt with the situation. The scholarships include a $1,000 academic scholarship given to one student a year to attend a John Hopkins program in the summer for three weeks for advanced studies in such areas as astronomy or physics.This was followed by an additional scholarship for needy kids who can't afford to go to school sponsored events.The school is given the latitude to do with it as they see fit. I trust them to make good decisions. It is now funded permanently. Income from a donation I made to a charitable foundation will fund it in perpetuity. I spoke to the school board in New York when setting up the fund, and they were very thankful, appreciative, sensitive and responsive.

What I would tell anyone going through this process is don't get upset when people talk about their grandchildren. I don't anymore. It's not in the consciousness of people around you that talking about grandchildren bothers you. Grandchildren is on the list of items I'll never have. My two step-sons may eventually have children, but I will never have direct grandchildren. I am just not letting it overwhelm me. You'll always hear others talk about grandchildren. Tune it out if you must, but don't get upset.

I live life on the short term. With the death of my son, I don't have a long term vision for my life anymore. But I did buy nursing home insurance.

Observations of Bernie

Seeing your child die in a sudden death is certainly not something you ever forget. For Bernie, it took him a long time to get through the depression and resume his life. But when he did, he found that time, medicines, doctors and a few organizations were of great help to him. He emphasizes the importance of good leadership for all self-help groups. Some leaders are not good at talking to parents, some groups are deep into religion. Others just may turn you off because you find it difficult to relate to the people in them for various reasons. Divisiveness within the group at how it should operate can also be detrimental to parents seeking help. Parents don't want to hear constant bickering from those running the group. You must feel comfortable in these groups for them to be productive for you.

Bernie found that because Parents of Murdered Children dealt with anger, and he felt much anger towards the pilot of the helicopter, this was a good group for him, as was Compassionate Friends who taught him to start focusing on helping others. Depending on how your child died may determine what group you would like to join or even start in your area. He encourages subscribing to Alive Alone and attending In Loving Memory conventions. All current groups were started by parents like Bernie who found a need existed. If you believe your situation is unusual, you may want to look into starting your own bereavement group. As Bernie says, "Being involved made me look at life differently."

Bernie has had many careers in his lifetime from a mail order and tax businesses to insurance and engineering. Besides a law practice in the near future, he and his wife wrote a "how-to, he said, she said" book on the process of how they ended up living in Louisville, Kentucky. He believes baby boomers will be looking for a better quality of life, and he has found it in Kentucky.

25

A Final Thought…

"Nothing can bring you peace, but yourself."

Ralph Waldo Emerson

An unknown author once wrote, *"I liken my grief to the bird with a broken wing. She never soared so high again, but her song was so much sweeter."* So it is with the grief of all parents. You will never know the happiness you once knew. It becomes a different joy, filled with compassion, courage and conviction that life is worth living and a desire to be of help to others.

You may not have the future you looked forward to when your child was born, but now there are new goals to achieve and a determination to make your 'song' as good as it can be in a world without your child. It is an opportunity to give back, to honor your child and to like yourself better.

This doesn't mean you'll never hurt again or that you will ever get over it completely. Trust your own timetable for healing, feel whatever you want to feel and grow in the process. In turn, your 'song' will enable you to reach new heights you never dreamed were possible.

Part 3

Photos of the Children

Marcy, 27, just before her marriage

Joe and Wanda's children, Afton and Dusty, the first day of school 1991

Sally's son Aaron with his father at 8th grade graduation

Helene's daughter, Sheryl, performing for charity at 23-years-old

Nat's son, Brian

Bernie and son, Robert, relaxing at home

Karl's son, Dave

Pat and Wayne's son, Stephen, 3

Nancy's son, Craig, at college

Diana's son, Jimmy

Pat and Wayne's daughter Stephanie, 7, getting ready for a dance recital

Bridie and Paul's son, Thomas

Celeste's daughter, Jennafer

Maryanne's daughter, Susan (right), with her sister, Sharon

Bridie and Paul's son, Paul Jr.

Maxine's son, Matthew, on his 21st birthday

Bev and Wayne's daughter, Jennifer at her graduation

Kathy's son, Jay

Bonnie and son, Justin

This is the AIDS quilt for Marion's son John.

Veronica's son, Michael (right), Jason (left) and Michael's other son, Channing, celebrating his birthday

Part 4

Resources

Resources

"If I can stop one heart from breaking, I shall not live in vain."

Emily Dickinson

Each of these organizations can direct you to local chapters.

Alive Alone, Inc.
11115 Dull Robinson Road
Van Wert, OH 45891
Phone: 419-238-1091
Email: alivalon@bright.net
Web site: www.alivealone.org

Bi-monthlynewsletters, networking system, books, videos, cassette tapes for bereaved parents, professionals and support group leaders.Helps parents cope with the death of their only child or all of their children. Bi-annual conferences are held where experts guide bereaved parents, hold workshops and educate professionals on how best to support these parents.

American Society of Suicidology (AAS)
5221 Wisconsin Ave., NW
Washington, DC 20015
Phone: 202-237-2280
FAX: 202-237-2282

Email: info@suicidology.org
Web site: www.suicidology.org

Supplies information to lead families of suicide victims to local resources such as survivor's groups.

Bereaved Parents U.S.A.
Box 95
Park Forest, IL 60466
Phone: 708-748-7672
Email: presidentBPUSA@aol.com
Web site: www.bereavedparentsusa.org

Provides network of peer support groups, newsletters and special help for parents, grandparents and siblings. Holds yearly conferences.

Bereavement Services
Gundersen Lutheran Medical Foundation
1900 South Avenue
LaCrosse, WI 54601
Phone: 608-775-4747 or 1-800-362-9567
FAX: 608-775-5137
Email: berserve@gundluth.org
Web site: www.bereavementservices.org

The training of healthcare professionals on how to care for bereaved parents when a loss occurs.

The Candlelighters Childhood Cancer Foundation
P.O. Box 498
Kensington, MD 20895
Phone: 301-962-3520 or 1-800-366-CCCF

FAX: 301-962-3521
Email: staff@candlelighters.org
Web site: www.candlelighters.org

For parent support of children who have or who have had cancer. Worldwide. No dues. Free bimonthly newsletter. Philosophy is that "It is better to light one candle than to curse the darkness."

The Compassionate Friends
Box 3696
Oak Brook, IL 60522
Phone: 630-990-0010 or 1-877-969-0010
FAX: 630-990-0246
Web site: www.compassionatefriends.org

International group welcoming bereaved parents of all ages. No pressure to talk; just listening to each other's story is okay. Volunteer organizations with over 650 chapters in the country. No dues, just be there for meetings.

First Candle/SIDS Alliance
1314 Bedford Ave. #210
Baltimore, MD 21208
Phone: 1-800-221-7437 or 410-653-8226
Email: info@firstcandle.org
Web site: www.firstcandle.org

For parents, caregivers and researchers. They work to fight infant mortality from SIDS and stillbirth. Counselors are available.The other organization is SIDS Educational Services, Inc. at 1-877-weloveyou, which does a lot of peer and professional counseling and has books.

MISS Foundation
P.O. Box 5333
Peoria, AZ 85385-5333
Phone: 623-979-1000
FAX: 623-979-1001
Email: info@missfoundation.org
Web site: www.misschildren.org

Provides immediate and ongoing support to families in crisis after the death of their child.

Mothers Against Drunk Driving (MADD)
511 E. John Carpenter Freeway
Suite 700
Irving, TX 75062
Phone: 1-800-GET-MADD
FAX: 972-869-2206
Web site: www.madd.org

Educates the public about the dangers of drinking and driving. Works to get stronger laws passed against drunk drivers. Quarterly newsletter.

National Association of People with AIDS
8401 Colesville Road,
Suite 750
Silver Springs, MD 20910
Phone: 240-247-0880
FAX: 240-247-0574
Email: info@napwa.org
Web site: www.napwa.org

Educates the public and provides services needed for those afflicted with AIDS. Can refer people to additional sources of help.

National Hospice and Palliative Care Organization
1700 Diagonal Rd, Suite 625
Alexandria, VA 22314
Phone: 703-837-1500
FAX: 703-837-1233
Email: nhpcoinfo@nhpco.org
Web site: www.nhpco.org

Provides individual help as well as group therapy to bereaved. Books and information for bereaved of all ages.

National Sudden Infant Death Foundation
2 Metro Plaza, Suite 205
8240 Professional Pl.
Landover, MD 20785
Phone: 301-322-2620
FAX: 301-322-9822

Helps parents deal with the shock and grief of losing their babies to SIDS and connects those parents. Provides information and counseling services. Bimonthly free newsletter to all SIDS parents.

National Tay-Sachs and Allied Diseases Association, Inc.
2001 Beacon St.
Suite 204
Brighton, MA 02135
Phone: 1-800-906-8723
FAX: 617-277-0134

Email: info@ntsad.org
Web site: www.ntsad.org

Helps parents with literature, emotional support and talking to parents with similar experiences.

Parents of Murdered Children
100 E. 8th Street, B-41
Cincinnati, OH 45202
Phone: 513-721-LOVE
FAX: 513-345-4489
Email: natlpomc@aol.com
Web site: www.pomc.com

Puts grieving parents in touch with each other. Chapters all over the United States for support and to be with those who will listen and understand.

National Share Office
Saint Joseph's Health Center
300 First Capitol Dr.
St. Charles, MO 63301
Phone: 636-947-6164
FAX: 636-947-7486
Email: share@nationalshareoffice.com
Web site: www.nationalshareoffice.com

Provides information for families who have lost babies through miscarriage, stillbirth, ectopic pregnancy or newborn death. SHARE has bimonthly newsletter written by parents and professionals. Provides information on other support groups.

SADD, Inc.
Students Against Destructive Decisions
Box 800
Marlboro, MA 01752
Phone: 1-877-SADD-INC
FAX: 1-508-481-5759
Email: info@SADD.org
Web site: www.saddonline.com

Students helping peers to resist consequences of destructive decisions and live safe, happy lives.

The Samaritans
Box 9086
Providence, RI 02940
Phone: 401-272-4044 (hotline)
Web site: www.samaritansri.org

For survivors of suicide victims. Provides self-help support. Meetings every week allow opportunity to ventilate feelings. Hotline also beneficial if not in Rhode Island.

Tragedy Assistance Program for Survivors, Inc. (TAPS)
1621 Connecticut Ave. NW
Suite 300
Washington, DC 20009
Phone: 1-800-959-TAPS
Email: info@taps.org
Web site: www.taps.org

Offers peer support and assists survivors who have lost a loved one in the line of military duty.

PART 5

Appendix

Comments and Notes from Parents and Friends...

"You have done a wonderful job of capturing all we had to say and we are touched that you would include us in your book."

Paul and Bridie

"I truly believe that you have captured the essence of my son as a living person along with my thoughts regarding his death."

Nat

"Your book has moved me deeply. My wife's best friend died so tragically. Reading her story takes me back to those dark melancholy times. More importantly, I view the book as a wake-up call. Too often it is human nature to take so much for granted. As a peripheral witness to this tragedy, and as one who was so impacted by it, this book reminds me to appreciate life. I would recommend it to not only bereaved parents but also to their relatives, neighbors and friends."

Marc

"God bless you in your wonderful work. Your child is leading you in a good path."

Kathy

"Thank you for asking me to participate in your very exciting project. I'm honored that you wanted my input."

Maxine

"Thank you for writing this book for all bereaved parents. What a wonderful memorial to your daughter. We are sure she is smiling down from heaven on you and so proud of what you are doing. We are very pleased and happy with what you wrote about our two children. In the observation you wrote, we couldn't have said it any better; it says just what we feel. God bless you and always keep you in His love and care."

Joe and Wanda

"I was feeling less than adequate in the sense of not having done enough in my son's memory. This book is just what I needed. It gave me a vehicle to tell our story and, hopefully, help others especially those dealing with loved ones with HIV and AIDS. This will remain in print long after I'm gone. That was exactly what I was looking for."

Marion

"Your book reaches out to everyone, those grieving the loss of a child, those helping someone who is grieving and all of us who face the eventuality of death. The harsh reality that life is so unpredictable made me appreciate my family and friends even more.

Kate

"I believe your book will help bereaved parents see how much they have in common with other bereaved parents and give a glimpse into how they might develop a meaningful future out of today's darkness."

Bernie

"Your book is full of hope, practical suggestions and insights for those of us who seek answers to the stifling sadness we feel when our children have died too soon."

Pat

"I found this book, with its insights of so many parents to be of great comfort to me. Knowing that I was not alone in this sea of uncertainty was so helpful."

Alison

"I commend you for taking your grief and turning it into something positive."

Danielle

Story Contributions

Dear Reader,

I am planning to do sequels to this book and need your help to get those stories told, to let people know that those suffering now will once again value each day and be able to live life to its fullest.

Have you personally ever suffered through the death of a child, a spouse, a best friend, a parent or a sibling?

The death of someone we love deeply can be overwhelming but eventually the pain does recede. We change, but we go on. Yet, there are many people who find it even difficult to greet each new day. They need to know that one day they will feel better and be able to cope with the loss. This is what I want to bring out in the sequels, that there is hope and a variety of techniques to guide us through our losses.

If you have a story to tell with the obstacles you faced, the healing process you went through, the ability you have to show others they are not alone in their suffering, and where you are now in your life, then I'd like to hear about it. For those who prefer not to do the writing, let me know, and I will interview you.

For those who are doing their own writing, stories may run any length, but you should aim for four to six pages, double-spaced. Type your name, address, phone, fax, and e-mail in the upper right-hand corner of the first page. You may submit your story in written form, and mail to me, or send it online to my email address: sfoxaz@hotmail.com using Microsoft Word and Times New Roman font. Along with the story send a one-paragraph biography, complete with address, phone and email and photo (not a professional one) of the person you are writing about to:

Sandy Fox
P.O. Box 25342
Scottsdale, AZ 85255-5342

Additional Book Order Form

Book copies can be obtained online or ordered at any commercial bookstore. If you want a personalized book signed by the author, send this form and a check or money order made payable to:

Sandy Fox
7407 E Pasaro Dr.
Scottsdale, AZ 85262

and provide the following information:

To whom personalized________________________________

Message____

____

____

Your name ____

Your address_______________________________________

City _______________State _____Zip ________ Phone__________

Mail book to:

Name____

Address____

City ________________State _____Zip ________ Phone__________

Cost of book is on the back cover.
Add applicable state tax to order
Shipping in the U.S. is $5.00 for the first book: $2.50 for each additional one to the same address.
International cost is $9.00 for the first book; $5.00 for each additional one to the same address.

Number of books __________at cost of _________each = __________

Applicable state taxes = __________

Shipping costs = __________

TOTAL ENCLOSED ____________

978-0-595-16118-8
0-595-16118-9